images of NATURE

images of NATURE

THE PHOTOGRAPHS OF THOMAS D. MANGELSEN

TEXT BY CHARLES CRAIGHEAD

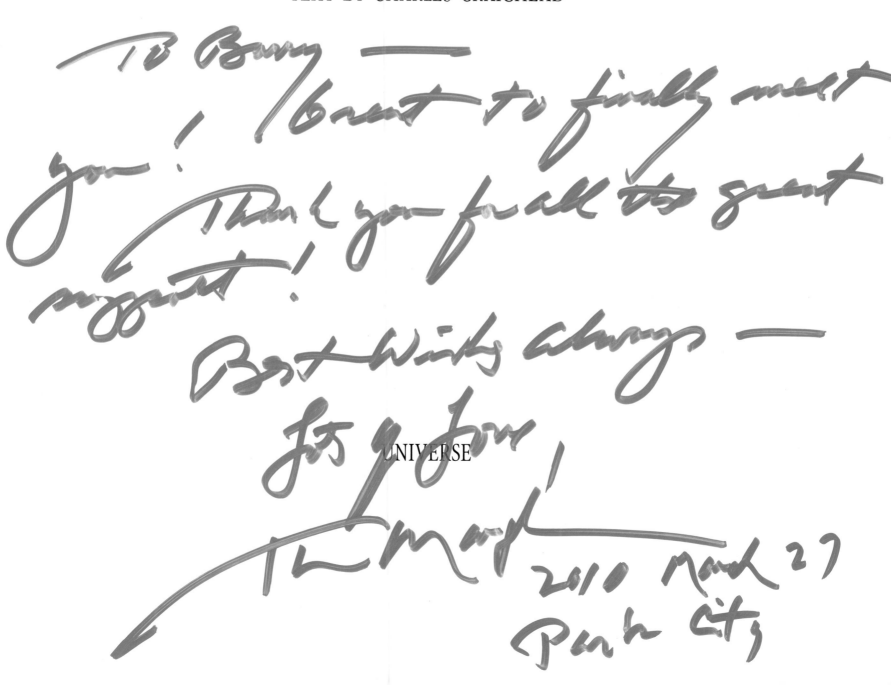

To Barry — ! Great to finally meet you! Thank you for all the great support! Best Wishes always — Tom Mangelsen

2010 March 27
Park City

UNIVERSE

I dedicate this book to my mother, Margaret Berenice, who gave me the understanding and the freedom to roam; to my father, Harold, who took me to the rivers and fields and showed me what was there; and to both of them for their unfailing support.

Published by Universe Publishing
A Division of Rizzoli International Publications, Inc.
300 Park Avenue South
New York, NY 10010
www.rizzoliusa.com

Images of Nature® is a registered trademark of Thomas D. Mangelsen, Inc., Omaha, Nebraska.
For information about reproduction rights to the photographs in this book or inquiries about limited edition prints contact: Images of Nature®, Post Office Box 45429, Omaha, NE 68145.

Design by Lee Riddell, Riddell Advertising & Design

08 05 03 02 01 00 99 97 96 94 92 89

Printed in China

ISBN-13: 978-0-7893-9986-1

Library of Congress Catalog Control Number: 2007906373

ACKNOWLEDGMENTS

· ·

I would like to thank the many people who made our book a reality.

My thanks to Charlie Craighead, whose words created beautiful images on their own. Hugh Levin, the publisher, whose support and confidence will always be appreciated and whose joyful attitude under deadline pressure will be remembered. Ron Palmer, the co-publisher, for his idea and initial interest in doing the book. Lee Riddell, for putting it all together, for her creative design and unending patience, and for caring so much. Ed Riddell, for his artistic eye and constant willingness to give needed advice.

I am also greatly indebted to my brother, David, who believed in my photography from the beginning and gave so much to make it all possible. Kathy Watkins and Dan Fulton, for their support and wonderful companionship in the field and for their organization and valuable assistance at the editing table. Margaret Murie, for her kind words and many years of inspiration. Paul Johnsgard, who took me under his wing in graduate school and first inspired me to pick up a camera. Nancy Kendrick, for convincing me that there are many choices in life. David Lenz, for his assistance and companionship on the Platte River. My grandfather, David Alexander, and my brothers, Bill and Hal, for their encouragement and valuable suggestions. Bert Kempers, for his confidence in me and for giving me my first photography job. Rod Drewien, Ernie Kuyt, and Gene Steffen, for their help in photographing the whooping cranes. My friends and guides in Africa, Yakub, Guchanja, Ali, and Peter.

Special appreciation is due to Robert Porath, Louise Lasley, Ellin Yassky Silberblatt, Dale Ramsey, Kerry Lamb, Maryellen Carlman, Lisa Bolton, Julie McIntyre, Marietta Lanphear, Magda Malachowski, Dale Upshaw, Ginna Bousum, Caroline Muller, Katherine Buell, Jerry Walker, Roy and Owen Gromme, Helen and Bob Grennan, Michael Fitzpatrick, Ellery and Donna Lenz, Wayne and Dorothy Schneider, Jon Stuart, Bob and Inger Koedt, Herman Weist, Richard O'Connor, Ellen Martin, Clarence and Dodie Stearns, and Bert and Meg Raynes.

My thanks also to the staff of Images of Nature galleries for giving me their support and the time that I dedicated to this book. In particular, I would like to thank Mary Rommelfanger, Shirley Nebel, Karen Digilio, Debbie Day, and Nancy Fredericks.

I also thank the U.S. Fish and Wildlife Service and the National Park Service for their help and cooperation.

To the many others who have helped in various ways and whom I have inadvertently forgotten and will remember after it is too late—thank you.

—*Thomas D. Mangelsen*

· ·

FOREWORD
images of the artist

. . . .

Consider a biologist turned photographer. Here is a heady combination— a double power. A biologist must have strong powers of observation, endless patience, a great interest in and sense of harmony with all living things, from elephants to the tiniest flower. All this the photographer must also have, along with knowledge of cameras, of lenses, and of lights and shadows. 🦢 Tom Mangelsen has all these traits, and among them I would rank his endless patience as the most important. 🦢 Some of Tom's pictures are almost unbelievable. In them it seems as if the subjects were cooperating in a conscious way. This has to be called "luck," I suppose, but I think the photographer must have a magical sensitivity that leads him to the right spot at the right moment. How else could it happen? 🦢 The shot of the Alaskan brown bear and the salmon on the cover of this book looks impossible, of course, so I am sure it must have sprung from that same magic—the combination of sharp observation and endless patience, with camera always on the ready. 🦢 I can't imagine the feeling of satisfaction that must warm the heart

. . . .

Trumpeter swans find warmth for their heads by tucking them under their wings in sub-zero temperatures. Mist rising from water nearby condenses and freezes on their plumage.

Trumpeter swans mate for life and return each spring to the same nesting territory where they reinforce their pair bond through courtship displays.

FRONTISPIECE
With his new antler growth covered in velvet, a bull elk drinks from a tributary of the Yellowstone River, where geothermally warmed water creates mist on cool summer mornings.

A fearless hunter of small rodents, the ermine—a short-tailed weasel in its white, winter phase—sometimes attacks prey as large as a snowshoe hare. The pure white fur will be shed for a brown coat in the spring.

of the photographer when he knows that he has captured not only the physique of an animal, but the animal in place in its habitat. I found myself gazing for a long time at the little winter ermine and feeling entranced by its at-home and serene "personality" in its proper setting.

To make this book a complete work of art, we have Charles Craighead's sensitive interpretations and comments. I have known Charlie all his life, and it is a real satisfaction to read his sympathetic words.

Tom and Charlie have given us an abiding delight. This book will take you all over the world. Turn the pages with joy.

And be thankful for patient people!

—*Margaret E. Murie*

Margaret E. Murie is one of North America's most respected voices in the effort to preserve wilderness. She spent nearly forty years living in the remote regions of the Rocky Mountains and Alaska studying wildlife with her husband, the renowned biologist and wilderness spokesman Olaus Murie. Her concern for the natural world has inspired three generations of naturalists.

CONTENTS

INTRODUCTION
images of an interior landscape

I n the first, faint light of a fifteen-degree winter morning, photographer Tom Mangelsen straps on his snowshoes and starts through deep snow toward a tree-lined riverbank, where mist rises slowly into the air. He carries a heavy tripod with a camera and a telephoto lens and a backpack filled with film, lenses, and spare batteries. Another camera hangs around his neck. His coat pockets bulge with extra gloves, smaller wide-angle lenses, binoculars, and a daily journal. His breath condenses and freezes on his collar. From a bridge a mile upstream Mangelsen has observed river otters catching fish the past two mornings. Photographs of otters are needed for a pending magazine article, but he also hopes to get an image good enough for a limited-edition print. He is headed for the bend in the river where he last saw the otters and hopes to be set up before they arrive to fish. Just before the sun rises, he reaches the river and peers carefully over the snowy riverbank at the water. No otters are in sight. Finding a spot where he can set up the tripod where only the long lens will be

Dense thickets of willow grow in the moist bottom-land soil of a mountain val-ley. The fast-growing shrubs are browsed back each year by wintering moose, and they are a favored food of the beavers that flood the thickets with their dams.

Banking sharply to dive after a salmon, a mature bald eagle displays the white head that inspired its name. The distinctive white feath-ers appear when the eagles are four or five years old.

CONTENTS
One of the most graceful of flyers, a herring gull hovers effortlessly in the wind while exploring the shoreline for food.

Winging from one feeding spot to another, trumpeter swans give their loud, hornlike call. The swans may winter near their northern nesting grounds if there is sufficient open water.

visible from the water, he waits in the morning stillness. Soon a raven calls from its roost in a spruce tree, and then a small flock of goldeneyes whistles past. The river community has come to life.

Mangelsen spends the morning waiting patiently for the otters to show up. Across the river, only a hundred feet away, he can see their tracks and the remains of fish from yesterday. He knows otters can cover miles of river in their daily travels and could appear at any time, and he thinks of what he missed the last two mornings when he was unable to snowshoe out to the river. While he waits, he takes a few pictures of a bald eagle circling in the distance. The morning sky is dramatic, but he won't know if he has caught the bird in a majestic pose until the film is processed; gloved hands and an eyepiece fogged by cold make the exact timing of the shutter release difficult.

By ten o'clock the otters still have not shown up, and the beautiful morning light has given way to harsh winter sky. Mangelsen packs up and mentally schedules himself to try again the next morning. Having the rest of the day to photograph, he thinks about other nearby possibilities for wildlife that would be productive in late afternoon or evening light. He starts slowly downstream, watching and listening from the riverbank. He decides to work his way to an oxbow bend in the river, where he suspects the otters may have their den in an old muskrat burrow. There, too, waterfowl congregate on the calm, open water, and other wildlife find shelter in the surrounding willows and forest. Even in the bright light of midday there may be chances for good images along the water's edge and in the open shadows of the trees.

After snowshoeing slowly for a half-mile along the river, Mangelsen hears the deep, hornlike call of trumpeter swans coming from downstream. The anxious sound indicates that they are in flight, so he kneels and readies his camera, focusing on the far bend in the river and quickly selecting a shutter speed and aperture. Then four of the huge, white swans fly gracefully around the bend and head toward him. He begins firing his motor-driven camera in short sequences, critically focusing and adjusting the composition as the swans approach. Knowing they will rise and turn when they see him, he steadies himself and waits until their formation and the position of their broad wings are right before shooting the last few frames. As they bank away from him into blue sky, he finishes the roll with a series of images of the swans in closeup.

To the southwest there is a wall of blowing snow as a small local storm moves out of the mountains and across the valley. Mangelsen estimates he will meet the storm at the oxbow bend and, still hoping to find the otters, visualizes a photograph of dark otters in a brief, driving snow. He short-cuts through a stand of old cottonwoods and young spruce trees, stopping to eat lunch on a fallen cottonwood and waiting for the light to improve as the snowstorm approaches. While he eats, he watches mountain chickadees flitting in the trees and hears a downy woodpecker rattling in the dead bark

A downy woodpecker's stiff tail holds it erect as it drills for insect larvae, eggs, and cocoons.

of one of the cottonwoods. He knows he already has better images of these birds than he could get in today's light, so he just sits still and watches, enjoying the company of the birds.

Out of the corner of his eye he sees a flash of white and turns to see an ermine, the white, winter phase of a weasel, standing boldly on the other end of the log. The little weasel is unafraid and curious, but it rarely stops long enough in its hunt for food to have its picture taken. Mangelsen slowly reaches for the camera resting on his pack and is surprised when the ermine stays put. He quickly takes a few shots and, when the ermine still doesn't flee, he leans forward to compose a new background. The ermine bounds off the log, and Mangelsen follows to the base of a dense spruce tree where the ermine dives into a dark hollow. When it reappears a second later, Mangelsen is focused and waiting, and he finishes the roll of film before the animal turns and runs. Excited about the unexpected good luck, Mangelsen leaves for the oxbow with the exposed film tucked safely in his shirt pocket.

When he arrives at the water's edge, the afternoon light is beginning to improve. Light snow is falling, and sunlight is burning through a corner of the storm, giving color and depth to the surroundings. The only thing missing is the otters. Mangelsen sets up and waits. The sky and scenery continue to look better, so he starts taking pictures of the landscape with its storm, river reflections, and falling snow.

Finally, as the western sky turns pink and the temperature starts to drop, he sees the familiar shapes of the otters working their way upriver, swimming porpoise-like, diving below and arcing above the surface. He watches in frustration as the otters seem to dawdle deliberately, as the light fades, and he constantly checks his light meter and makes adjustments in preparation. Just as the light drops below the limit for a shutter speed fast enough to freeze the otters in their mercurial activities, they slide up onto the ice barely fifty feet away. The last otter out of the water carries a whitefish, and the animals devour it, then roll in the snow and wrestle playfully. Mangelsen can only watch with mixed feelings of fascination and frustration; the photographer in him tries to think of a way to get something other than a dark, blurry picture, while the naturalist in him enjoys the intimate encounter. The otters move off the ice and swim upriver, and Mangelsen packs his cameras.

Snowshoeing back to his car, he reviews his day's images and reminds himself to feel positive about the results despite the disappointing conclusion. He regrets missing the otters by only a few minutes, but the pictures of the ermine and the landscape and storm at the oxbow will definitely be good, and the swans and the bald eagle are possible prints. He has been doing this long enough to know that he should not worry about missed opportunities, especially with a wild and free-roaming subject like wildlife. It also presents a challenge to return tomorrow to try for the images he saw while the otters played in fading light.

Most professional wildlife photographers would have difficulty pinpointing exactly when or how it became a career. Once it did, few would

A Canada goose sets its wings for a landing on the open water of a river, where it will roost for the night.

willingly change their way of life. Many wildlife photographers have more training in the natural sciences than in anything technical, and few have any formal photographic training. Tom Mangelsen followed a typically circuitous route to arrive at his occupation. Like most artists, his early life's experiences shaped his future, even if he wasn't aware of it until later. He had just kept following what he felt was the most personally rewarding path.

"I grew up along the Platte River and in the sandhill country of western Nebraska," he says, "spending all my spare time duck and goose hunting with my father or just following the braided channels of the Platte to see what I could see. The sandhill country and its wildlife had a great influence on me. When I graduated from college and faced the reality of making a living, I tried to find a way to combine a profession with my love of being outdoors. Medicine seemed like a challenging career that might eventually give me that flexibility. But it didn't take long to see that as a rather backward approach, so I looked for a more direct way to support myself by doing what I liked, being in the company of wildlife. I transferred my educational direction from medicine and business to wildlife research. At the same time, I found myself enjoying the few art courses I was taking more than many of my wildlife studies."

Mangelsen began taking photographs when he was out in the field. He had grown to appreciate the artistic value of a scene, whether he saw a beautiful bird or a favorite landscape. Without any training he began trying to record what he saw for his own satisfaction. He had no intention of finding a career in photography or art, but was inspired to photograph the subjects he knew best; waterfowl, especially birds in flight became his main passion. This proved to be a valuable training exercise and a major step toward making more complex compositions of wildlife within a landscape.

"Around then, I broke away from the family business and school and went west. I got a job as a cinematographer making educational biology films in Boulder, Colorado, and continued with my still photography. I kept seeing photographs of waterfowl and other birds that I thought I could improve upon, and finally printed some of my own images for a summer art fair. I sold two. Being young and naive about the realities of a photography career, I decided to try it on my own."

Mangelsen now travels seven months of the year to various locations around the world, following the migrations and seasonal concentrations of wildlife. There are many well-known points of congregation for wildlife, like Alaska's McNeil River for brown bears or Nebraska's Platte River for sandhill cranes, but Mangelsen also has his own locations where few if any other photographers go. It is in these places that he gets images of familiar animals against new and distinctive backgrounds and finds wildlife subjects that are rarely photographed. One of the features of Mangelsen's work is his depiction of smaller and less dramatic species in compositions that bring out their beauty and character. One such image is that of two kestrels, or sparrow hawks, the smallest of the falcons and a common sight along roadsides and

Cold autumn weather will send this young red-tailed hawk on its southward migration when snow covers the ground and prey becomes scarce. The dark-color phase of the red-tailed hawk is characteristic of the mountains of the North American West.

on telephone wires throughout the country.

"It was late spring, and a friend and I were in the Lamar Valley in the north end of Yellowstone Park," Mangelsen recalls. "The Lamar is a good place to find grizzlies feeding after they've come out of hibernation, so we were working our way up the valley, checking the hillsides with binoculars. At one point we heard the characteristic *killy, killy, killy* of the kestrel and saw the silhouettes of a pair of kestrels landing in a grove of cottonwoods. I decided to investigate, and found the pair defending a nesting territory. It had snowed earlier that morning, and there was snow plastered to the limbs. The sky was overcast.

"We watched the birds for several hours and became fascinated with the daily lives of a pair of kestrels. First we saw the male defend his new territory against another male kestrel by attacking it and knocking it off its perch, grabbing the intruder on the breast with his talons. Both birds plummeted to the snowy ground with the defending male on top, and only when the intruding male accepted its subordinate role did the defending male let it go. Shortly after that a red-tailed hawk landed in the grove, and even though it was many times the size of the kestrel, the little falcon drove it away with repeated dive-bombing and loud cries. All the while the female was searching through the trees for a nesting hole. Between bouts of defending his territory the male would swoop down and catch mice at the base of a spruce tree and present them to the female. In the middle of all this activity, the female would periodically call to the male, and they would mate and then rest. It was during one of these periods of rest, when the male was looking at the female and yawning, that I made my favorite image. It was a stark scene, with the wintry white sky, the dead tree limbs covered with snow, and then the two splashes of color. Graphically, it would become one of the strongest images of my career, and it reminds me of one of my most interesting days in the field. It is these special, unexpected days that make wildlife photography such an extraordinary experience."

Although Mangelsen would not trade his career for any other, the occupation that seems from the outside to be a perfect job is in reality a competitive and often frustrating way of making a living. The time spent actually photographing becomes the reward for endless hours of travel, getting permits, researching, and waiting. Often the job is a narrowing-down process, gradually working toward finding the best subject and best background. Only after all this can the artistic side take over. Mangelsen recalls his photograph of a puffin with its bill full of fish, which he made along the coast of Maine during the puffin's nesting season, a brief period when the birds come to rocky coastlines from the open sea: "The actual exposure of the film can be almost anticlimactic in a case like this, when I learned the life cycle of the birds, where they came to shore, where they nested, what times of day they fished, and, finally, where individual birds would habitually land before ducking into their burrows."

From the beginning, when he was primarily photographing waterfowl

The berries of the mountain ash remain on the tree through the winter and are an important food source for late-nesting birds like the cedar waxwing.

and other birds, Mangelsen adhered to his biological training and made sure that the scene was correct, that the animal was doing what came naturally and that it was portrayed in its normal habitat. This led to his frequent use of the local climate to underscore the conditions in the animal's environment. He began to turn fog, clouds, rain, and snow into essential elements of the photograph. "I realized I couldn't wait for the sun to shine for dramatic lighting and that animal activity went on whether it was raining, snowing, or blowing. I began to find that the animals were remarkable reflections of the mood of the weather by their positions and appearance. They also tended to be less concerned about me if their activities were strongly influenced by the weather. There was a big difference between a bird sitting on a limb in bright summer sunshine and the same bird hunkered down on a frozen branch with its feathers puffed up in twenty-below-zero weather."

From that development, Mangelsen proceeded to incorporate more and more of the environmental conditions into his scenes until, in some instances, the bird or mammal became a minor part of the image. Such landscapes of wildlife habitat may contain only a small silhouette or a distant but recognizable animal shape, but nevertheless convey all the intense feeling of a close-up action photograph.

Still, Mangelsen may be best known for his natural depiction of animal behavior. He finds animals feeding, calling a mate, or caught in a posture that suggests impending flight. He relies on his training as a biologist to recognize and record bits of behavior that accentuate the images' naturalism. His picture of a sea otter floating on its back sleeping shows the otter's habit of wrapping itself in kelp to keep the tides from drawing it out to sea, and his photographs of flocks of bright waxwings clustered on a mountain ash tree were recorded when the birds made their annual search for late-ripening berries in sub-zero temperatures.

Anticipating behavior and where it will lead an animal in relation to a background is what gives Mangelsen the compositions he wants. Years of watching and learning the movements of animals has developed his ability to bring together the photographic process and natural behavior at the chosen scene. Many of his images are made when an animal moves into the camera's view, as if on a set, rather than when the animal is followed until it holds still. Mangelsen's images thus give the impression of being the view of an invisible bystander in a natural drama. This attribute comes from taking time not only to learn the habits of the subject, but also to allow it to become accustomed to an outside presence.

It all derives from patience, a quality Mangelsen learned by hunting with his father along the Platte River. "If you could hunt ducks and geese with Harold," he remarks, "you could wait for anything. Watching all day for an eagle to catch a salmon is nothing compared to sitting in Dad's goose blind. Patience usually has its reward, but in photography you have to know what that reward is going to be. You have to do more than just sit somewhere and wait for something to happen. When I was in Denali photographing grizzlies

Wading gracefully through their marshy home, black-necked stilts feed in the shallow water. Among shore-birds, stilts have the longest legs in proportion to body size.

as they hunted arctic ground squirrels, I saw the possibility for an image that would be worth waiting for. Even though the chance was remote and it would take a lot of luck, I knew it was a matter of spending the time to get the picture I wanted of a huge and powerful grizzly closing in on a small ground squirrel. The action may be brief and hard to see, but I hoped that eventually a squirrel might flee in the open, and in the right direction and distance from the bear, to make it a chase. I was lucky, but I had to wait and work for it."

The most beneficial use of his wildlife biology work is his understanding of the relationships of animals and plants and of how to find one subject in conjunction with another. Because his subject matter is free and wild, there are no guarantees that a trip for a specific animal will be productive. So Tom must know which other species can be found in a given vicinity and be prepared if his primary subject is not accessible or if the arrival or departure of a migratory species has not been as expected. One of his more popular prints is that of a robin—not really considered a great subject by most wildlife photographers—that appeared while Mangelsen was waiting for a flock of Bohemian waxwings to move to a berry-laden tree near his camera. The result was an image revealing the robin as a wild thrush instead of as a familiar lawn decoration. Another time, while waiting for fog to lift from a marsh so that he could look for cranes, Mangelsen watched black-necked stilts wading in the dense mist. He could barely see them through the viewfinder but started photographing anyway, hoping something recognizable would come through the thick fog. His result was a beautiful, eerie image of two black-necked stilts stepping delicately in the mist.

Working in national parks and wildlife sanctuaries has imbued in Mangelsen a strong belief in the need for the conservation of natural resources. He actively supports the efforts of many groups and donates his photographic skills when possible. "It's not just a matter of trying to protect the basis for my occupation by helping wildlife," he says. "My photography is a way of showing people what's out there. If I can get people to feel what I do when I see a great gray owl or a loon, then it's that much easier to convince them we need to protect these things. If my photography career had not developed I'd be out there with the same goal, but possibly painting, sculpting, or doing research."

Mangelsen keeps in contact with many wildlife research projects and works jointly with biologists to promote studies of rare or endangered species. In 1984 he filmed and helped produce a National Geographic television special, *Flight of the Whooping Crane,* which depicted the migration of the rare birds and the efforts to save them from extinction. He found the film especially rewarding to make. "The whooping crane was historically found along the Platte during migrations from their wintering grounds to nesting areas in the north. I grew up with sandhill cranes on the Platte but never saw whoopers. It was a great satisfaction to be able to contribute to the effort to make people aware of the beautiful cranes and of the scientists' efforts to bring them back

Whooping cranes hovered on the edge of extinction for years, but recent protection and management have brought a gradual comeback for one of the rarest and most celebrated birds. In 1941, only fifteen of these cranes were known to exist.

Sandhill cranes mass for their evening roost in the shallow Platte River, where the current discourages predators. The Platte and surrounding land is critical for migrating cranes to gain strength and reaffirm pairs.

from near-extinction. I feel the real purpose of my work is to convince people to save what natural beauty and wildlife we still have."

In wind-driven snow, Tom Mangelsen's camera sits on its tripod protected by a waterproof cover, but the photographer huddles behind a snowdrift to escape the brunt of the storm. Still, the cold powder sifts down his neck and over his face. Watching a flock of waterfowl from the bridge, he had seen otters far downstream during a lull in the blizzard. So he had quickly loaded his pack and snowshoed out to the river. Now, as the storm closes in again and he has to sit unmoving, he begins to feel the chill. He thinks of a warmer coat left behind in the car and the thermos bottle of hot coffee forgotten on the seat. Then the chirping call of the otters reaches him, and as the sound seems to come closer on the wind, he peers over the snowdrift. There is nothing but blowing snow and the dark water of the river. The otters are out there, but only luck will bring a break in the storm when the animals arrive. Tom Mangelsen pulls his collar closer and wraps his arms over his knees—and he waits.

Sunset on the Pacific coast colors the sky over Monterey Bay, California.

The serrated edges of its bill keep a common puffin's catch of fish secure as it returns to its burrow nest. Puffins use their stubby wings as fins to "fly" under-water in pursuit of fish, and when they catch a fish it is pinched and then held until the bill is full.

WATERSIDE
images of coast and shoreline

· ·

Coastal life mirrors the cyclic tides and seasonal nature of the ocean. Animals appear and disappear in phenomenal numbers, migrating to breeding grounds or congregating for seasonal sources of food. There is a full range of life forms, from birds to fish to carnivorous mammals. There are colossal whales and microscopic plants, predators and prey. The sea tempers the air and nourishes plants, its influence pushing inland until mountains halt the flow of moisture. This is a rich zone of briny water and lush plant growth, of bounty and famine both. A brief squall moves from the open sea into a cold Alaskan bay. Dense sheets of rain march toward the shoreline, pushed by gusts of wind. The rain spatters unnoticed in the surf, pounds the sand, and washes salt spray from the beach vegetation. It carries far inland where it blurs the air and drips from great trees. After the storm, fog and a light rain fill the summer sky. From the swells of the sea a gray whale breaches and sounds. Its tail hangs in the air briefly, dripping sea water, then slips gracefully into the depths. A school of sockeye

· ·

Its seven-foot wingspan carries a bald eagle on a flight along the Alaskan coast in search of fish.

salmon mills in the deep water offshore, waiting for the tides to push them up into the stream of their origin. As fingerlings they entered salt water four years ago to begin their transformation into sleek sea creatures. They explored the fathoms of the oceans, and some carry scars from seals and sea otters or from predatory fish. The weak have been sifted from the school. Now the salmon return to breed and die in their native fresh water. They no longer eat, intent only on surviving the shock of fresh water and the upstream battle to calm pools. Their powerful bodies are changing once again, now growing humped and hooked and turning crimson. With a tidal surge, the school swarms up into the glacial stream.

On the dead snag of a huge coastal spruce, a bald eagle sits hunched in the downpour. Instinctively it scans the dense coastal vegetation and meandering stream, watching for prey. A dark shadow moving in the stream below causes the eagle to sit erect and focus sharply; the school of sockeyes moves in deep water along one shore where the overhanging vegetation protects them. They burst from cover into a wide, shallow riffle, headed for the deeper water. Their dorsal fins break the surface as they splash through the shallows, and the eagle leans into the wind. Becoming airborne, it tucks into a long, shallow dive that levels out just above the water. Its powerful feet and sharp talons reach forward to pull a thrashing salmon out of the water, and the eagle carries it heavily across the river to a gravel bar.

The eagle's arrival frightens a flock of western sandpipers, which lift noisily into the air and zigzag downstream to the beach. They settle at the water's edge and begin following the ebb and flow of the surf, searching for food in the exposed shallows. The eagle feeds on its salmon, then flaps upward, slowly circling over the stream. It joins another eagle drifting high over snowfields and glaciers above the steep coastal valley. Soon there will be thousands of eagles drawn to the spawning salmon.

The leading salmon press on, unaware of the feast in their wake. Their numbers diminish as they encounter river otter and mink and then the brown bears that wait in the last cascades before the spawning beds. The migrating salmon will finally reach the headwaters where, once their eggs are laid in the gravel, their life cycle will end. Then the decomposing bodies of the sockeyes will nourish new life as they begin to drift downstream to the sea.

The streamlined flukes of a gray whale drip sea water, and its tail hangs briefly in the air as it dives after surfacing to breathe.

Peering from the shadows
of its marshy feeding
ground, a great egret hunts
its prey. The beautiful
nuptial plumes of the great
egret, grown only during the
breeding season, were once
in such demand by millin-
ers that egrets were hunted
to near extinction.

Its long bill ready to strike,
a great egret waits for a
movement in the water to
reveal its prey of fish or
crustaceans.

The hermit thrush nests on the ground in the moss and grass of coastal forests and thickets. It is considered to have one of the most beautiful songs of any North American bird.

Bizarre facial patterns mark the harlequin, a small duck that nests along turbulent mountain streams and winters in stormy coastal water.

FOLLOWING PAGES
Sunrise finds a young white-tailed deer poised where it has come to feed on plants at the water's edge.

With two of its young on its back and the rest lined up behind, a common merganser crosses a turbulent stretch of Brook's River in Alaska. The fish-eating merganser is attracted by the remains of salmon caught by brown bears.

A sow Alaskan brown bear brings her cubs to a traditional food source—the annual run of salmon to their spawning grounds—to learn to fish.

ALASKAN BROWN BEARS
notes from the field

At daybreak every morning for a week, I would poke my head out of my tent and look east across Naknek Lake to see what weather the Gulf of Alaska had sent, and to see if there were bears on the shoreline. Before crawling out of the tent I would also look up and down the trail that passed between me and the lakeshore to make sure I didn't come face to face with a bear in the dim light.

If it was not pouring rain—and it was likely to be, since this area receives over 200 inches a year—and if the trail was clear of bears, I would eat a cold breakfast of fruit and pack my lunch, my cameras, lenses, film, and tripod, then walk the two miles to Brooks Falls.

The trail to the falls winds through dense forest. Visibility is limited, and the path has been well worn by the many animals that use it. Fresh claw marks and bear scat from last night's traffic could be seen every hundred yards or so. It was a good idea to advertise your presence on the trail, so I whistled and made up songs. When I ran out of tunes, I would talk aloud to myself or to the "shadow bear." Anyone not knowing about all the bears would think I was "the happy camper." But whether it made me self-conscious or not, it was better to appear crazy than to meet a thousand-pound brown bear by surprise.

I could hear the falls from a half-mile away. Each day when I crested the last hill and reached the viewing platform, the scene overlooking the falls was different. Some days there were no bears in sight. Other days there seemed to be bears everywhere; there might be two below the platform, one or two in the deep pools below the falls and on the rocks across the river, and possibly one or two standing in the water above the falls. Each bear had a different fishing technique, used with varying degrees of success, depending on age and experience. There was one older bear that snorkeled for fish, one huge bear called Scar Saddle (for the scars he got in a fishing dispute) who was successful in diving for fish, and several younger bears that splashed wildly without much luck. There were also several bears that waited patiently above the falls for the fish to come to them. It was this last group that I enjoyed watching most and envisioned as the best subjects. They would stand hour after hour waiting for a salmon to leap

*A brown bear patiently
waits for a salmon to
attempt to leap up the
cascade.*

*Sockeye salmon leap the
falls to reach spawning
grounds in shallow head-
waters. After laying and
fertilizing their eggs in
gravel beds, the fish die, and
their decomposition adds
nutrients to the stream
environment.*

notes from the field *(continued)*

the falls near enough to trap with their paws or grab in
their mouths.

The decisive moment for a photograph was that
millisecond between mouth opened and mouth closed.
The image would have to be tight enough to make a viewer
feel the spray from the cascading water, the slippery stones
under the bear's feet, and the rush of sockeye salmon against
his legs. To feel close enough to smell the great bear's
breath—that was the tension I wanted to capture. Timing,
light, exposure, composition, depth of field, shutter speed,
and luck would be more critical than usual.

I framed the bear, visualizing how it would look with
a salmon in the air, then realized that even without the
fish it was a strong and beautiful image of a patient bear.
Slow shutter speeds would abstract the cascading water
and isolate the motionless bear, so I experimented while
the bear and I both waited for the salmon to arrive. I passed
several hours, forgetting the wind and cold and wet, and
experimented with various exposures.

Other wildlife activity at the falls included a family of
merganser ducks feeding on the plentiful scraps of salmon
and fish eggs left by the bears. As they crossed the river
from scrap to scrap, all the young would try to ride across
the falls on their mother's back, but only a few would
fit. As the days passed, the ducklings rapidly grew larger,
so fewer and fewer would fit on her back. Some were
lost to glaucous-winged gulls or the strong current. It
seemed like a harsh place to raise ducklings barely the
size of a golf ball, but the mergansers had been lured by
the same plentiful salmon that brought the bears.

During brief periods when several salmon per minute
were jumping the falls and the mergansers were passing
by at the same time, I had a difficult time deciding which
to photograph. The ducks were easy and there was drama
in their crossings, but the bear and salmon image was a
real challenge. After a week I still wasn't sure I had gotten
the image I wanted of the catch. I had seen it several times,
which was special enough, but it all happened so fast,
and there were so many variables, that I couldn't be sure
if I had reacted quickly enough to capture it on film. I
did not know for certain until I saw the processed film
weeks later.

Caught in the split second before the jaws of a brown bear close around it, a sockeye salmon hangs helplessly in midair.

A shy bird of ponds and waterways, the green-backed heron can often be seen poised motionlessly watching for prey or moving cat-like through shallow water, one stealthy step at a time, grabbing small fish in its bill.

A black oystercatcher in Prince William Sound waits for a receding tide to uncover mussels and clams, which it pries open with the tip of its chisel-like bill. Catastrophic oil spills are especially devastating to the fragile intertidal zone and the birds that feed there.

Offshore rocks offer a harbor seal safe sunbathing in Monterey Bay.

After feeding on sea urchins and crabs, a napping sea otter wraps itself in the kelp of Monterey Bay to keep from drifting away. Tiny bubbles trapped in the otter's dense fur keep it warm and afloat.

PREVIOUS PAGES
A Louisiana, or tri-colored, heron watches for fish in tidal channels and marshes of the southern United States. The heron often hunts by running in shallow water or stirring the bottom with one foot to flush its prey.

*A ring-billed gull stretches
while waiting for afternoon
winds and tides to arrive so
it can hunt for food.*

Each spring, common puffins return to land from the open sea, then choose mates and dig their burrow nests on rocky headlands. When the young are fully grown, they are abandoned in the burrow, and the parents fly back out to sea.

Black-legged kittiwakes are
small, graceful gulls that
build deeply cupped nests
on sheer sea cliffs. They nest
in large colonies along the
northern coasts and on
offshore islands.

The moods associated with the meeting of the churning sea and the land would not be complete without the gulls that ride the winds of approaching storms.

FOLLOWING PAGES
Daisies growing along a lakeshore add their subtle color to the brief summer of northern Maine.

Loons, which nest on the islands and shorelines of pristine lakes, are considered a sign of undisturbed wilderness. Because they live on the fish of northern lakes, loons are susceptible to the contaminants in acid rain.

Distinct markings and a ruby eye distinguish the common loon. Loons have solid bones and dense bodies that enable them to sink below the surface without a ripple in pursuit of fish.

COMMON LOON
notes from the field

For some reason, like many people I have a special attraction to loons. Maybe it is their color and shape, their haunting call, or the wild regions of woods and water where they live. The Maine North Woods is one such region. There one finds an area that seems to be almost half water and half woods—a real maze of lakes, streams, marshes and forests cover the landscape. I wanted to see this country and photograph the loons, so my companion and fellow photographer Kathy Watkins and I did some research on the area and on the habits of the loons. Learning where to go, getting there, and setting up are often the biggest challenges of nature photography.

We went to one of the region's largest lakes. A gravel road took us to the shore, and there in the woods, chained to a tree, was the small fishing boat we had arranged to have as our transportation for the next five days. Our quarters, an old fishing shack, we were told, was "about a half-mile east of the stashed boat by way of an old logging road now grown over and hard to find, or a bit farther by boat, around some shallow, rocky shoals between a couple of small islands, around a point of land, and you're there."

Those directions and our pile of heavy gear made the longer route by boat sound like the easy way, and since we needed the boat to explore the lake anyway, we loaded it up. We piled in our camera gear, sleeping bags, tent, life vests, food, and our last four beers. I poured the mixture of gas and oil into the three-horsepower motor, jerked on the cord a dozen times, pushed the lever to reverse, and in a cloud of wonderful-smelling blue smoke we were off— just long enough to get our bow off the shore and hear the motor sputter to a stop. In the abrupt silence a scolding red squirrel seemed to taunt us from his tree. I untangled the mass of water lily roots cinched around the propeller, pulled on my rubber waders, and got out to pull the boat to deeper water. Feeling a rush of cold water on my left leg, I remembered the hole in my boot behind the knee. As far back as I can remember, it has seemed natural to have cold, wet feet, even with wading boots. My dad would say, "Just wiggle your toes."

Beyond the tangle of vegetation, we were on our way

The haunting, laughter-like
call of the common loon is
an unforgettable sound of
the northern wilderness.
Their wailing cries at night,
echoing across moonlit
lakes, gave rise to the
expression "crazy as a loon."

Seemingly able to walk on
water, a young white-tailed
deer bounds across the
shoals of a shallow lake.

notes from the field (continued)

at last, watching a beautiful sunset and what looked like
the silhouette of a loon in the distance on the mirrorlike
water. Loon country! Suddenly I heard the scraping of our
aluminum hull against the rocks and the pop of the propeller
jumping out of the water. I'd been here before: cold, wet
feet, water too shallow to motor the boat—it was another
Mangelsen adventure.

Kathy and I took turns pulling the boat toward a "hot
meal in our cabin in the woods." We passed by a half-
dozen islands before we found water deep enough to run
the motor. Slowly, we rounded point after point, squinting
into what seemed total darkness for a sign of our cabin.
By now we were wet and cold from our waists down,
the price of finding deeper water. (I remembered an
executive I had met in my gallery a week earlier; envious
of my career, he had wanted to trade jobs. *Now* I was
willing!) In such circumstances one learns a lot about a
traveling companion's personality. Anyone still able to
laugh, as Kathy was, is worth having along.

In desperation we fumbled in our packs and found
a flashlight. It was the small backpacker kind that campers
use to find a toothbrush at the bottom of their packs. Kathy
pointed it directly toward shore, which made us laugh,
because the beam of light barely reached the bow of the
boat. About the time we were ready to turn back, we saw
the cabin.

We built a fire to warm ourselves and dry our clothes.
Hungry, but too tired to cook, we celebrated reaching loon
country with a jar of pickled herring, crackers topped with
cheddar cheese, and one of the beers. We decided to leave
the bunk beds and mattresses to their present occupants,
which we took from the obvious signs to be packrats and
mice. We spread our sleeping bags out on the wooden
floor, turned off the lantern, and went to sleep.

I awoke an hour later as a mouse ran across my hand,
and I listened for a while to the nocturnal sounds of little
animals scurrying around the old fishing shack. Finally I
fell asleep again, only to be reawakened by a great gnawing
sound from outside the door. I slowly opened the screen
door and shone the flashlight onto the wooden steps. A
large brown, summer-coated snowshoe hare with huge
white feet was nibbling on the steps. It took one look

*In thick forest surrounding
a wilderness lake, a red
squirrel peers cautiously
from its tree home. Like
other animals of the north
that do not migrate or
hibernate, the squirrel
busily stores food for the
approaching winter.*

*A common loon chick
follows its parent through
the reflections of their
wilderness surroundings.
Chicks will often ride on the
adult's back since their own
downy feathers get easily
soaked.*

notes from the field *(continued)*

at me and hopped gently away. By now Kathy was awake and wondering what was going on. I told her, leaving out the part about the mouse running over my hand, and she immediately dragged her sleeping bag out the door to a grassy area in front of the cabin. Mosquitoes had invaded the woods as the evening breeze had died down, so at 4 a.m., shortly before daybreak, we pitched our tent in front of the cabin. As I drifted off to sleep, I wondered if there really were any loons on this lake. Thirty minutes later, at the first sign of daylight, I heard my answer— the unmistakable yodeling call of a pair of loons directly in front of our camp. It was as if they had come to greet us.

I hoped that the difficult part of this expedition was over and that I could get to work photographing loons. Eventually, Kathy and I did observe and photograph four different loon families!

We enjoyed our five days out on the lake, exploring its coves and the little streams that flowed into it. Every morning at sunrise, we would see amber-colored dots glowing on the far eastern shoreline. We discovered these to be white-tailed deer feeding on the succulent grasses in the shallows along the shore. We would see them only for the first half-hour of daylight, and then they would disappear. One day we rounded a point and saw one of the deer a hundred yards from shore. The sleek young buck with velvet antlers watched us as though he'd never seen a boat or humans before, then raised his tail and leaped gracefully through the water and back to cover. We each shot a series of pictures which, as often happens, turned out to be at least as special as those we had come for. I'll never forget the image of the largest bull moose I have ever seen, although I didn't get a picture of him. He was in a wooded cove at twilight, standing shoulder deep and raising his massive velvet-covered antlers out of the water as he fed on submerged plants. The loons, the deer, the moose, even the carpet of wild daisies around the shack, are not only on film, but etched in our memories. By the end of our stay on this wild northern lake, I had learned where the rocky shoals were, and I had no more thought of trading jobs with anyone.

FOLLOWING PAGES
Western sandpipers follow the Pacific coastline of Washington as they migrate north in the spring. These sandpipers will nest only along the coast of western and northern Alaska, but in winter will spread out from California to South America.

With its powerful feet and talons outstretched to pluck a salmon from the water, a bald eagle skims the calm surface of a spawning stream.

Sunlight accents the pure white feathers and yellow beak of a mature bald eagle as it rests in a spruce tree. From its high perch, the eagle watches for fish or other prey below.

Common puffins and
razorbills are gregarious
seabirds that nest in
colonies along rugged
northern coasts. Out at sea,
where they dive after fish,
the adult birds have been
observed as deep as sixty
feet underwater.

The surfbird seems not to notice spray or splashing water as it feeds along the line of surging sea water. In summer the surfbird flies high into the mountains of Alaska, where it nests far from water.

A brant feather lost in the late summer molt is all that remains of the migrating birds when the first autumn storm comes to the Alaskan coast.

*Migrating whimbrels gather
on the rocks of a Pacific
bay. The whimbrel is a
medium-sized curlew that
nests in the northern
tundra and winters as far
south as Chile.*

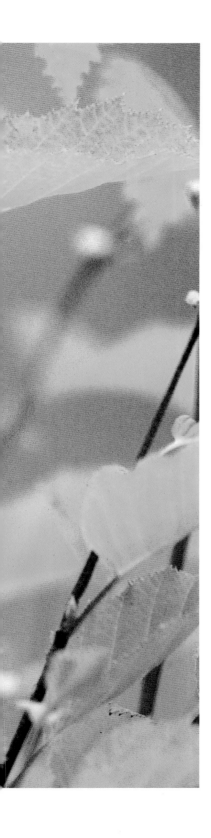

An arctic tern rests briefly before taking to the air again. In the course of nesting in the arctic and wintering in the seas of Antarctica, the arctic tern may fly up to 22,000 miles a year.

A familiar sound along Alaskan coasts is the call of the song sparrow coming from low, dense vegetation. The song sparrow prefers to live near water, and its various subspecies are found across the entire continent.

HIGHLANDS
images of mountain and forest

The deep red of mountain maple is one of the brightest autumn colors in the western mountains. Aspen trees, with their soft white bark, are just beginning to turn deep yellow.

With its feathers puffed up in minus-twenty-degree weather, a Bohemian waxwing displays the red, waxy tips of its wing feathers that give waxwings their name.

Where the granite spine of North America is exposed and weathered lies a world of dense pine forests, lakes, rivers, and sculptured peaks. The high country is a rich nesting and birthing ground in summer and a quiet land of snow and bare subsistence in winter. It is the retreat of plains animals displaced by man, the realm of the few remaining great predators and concentrated herds of prey. Here, ecological variety offers niches to countless shapes and sizes of life, from water lilies in glacier scoured ponds to mountain sheep on windy, high crags. In the brief flush of life that is the highland summer, colorful and delicate birds such as the mountain bluebird and western tanager arrive to nest and raise young. Seasons change quickly, and life adapts to the transformation of the landscape. When winter mantles the land, animals must move, adapt, or hibernate. Many do leave for warmer climates or lower elevations and find new winter food, others change their coloring for seasonal camouflage. Herds of grazing animals find open, windswept hillsides where the vegetation is cleared of snow. The

*Long metallic-purple
feathers spread over a white
throat mark the male
calliope hummingbird, the
smallest bird in North
America. Hummingbirds
must feed almost continu-
ally to fuel their metabolism,
but the males may become
dormant on cold nights to
conserve energy.*

*A spring snowstorm
greets the male mountain
bluebird, who arrives early
on his summer range to
claim a nesting territory.
The bluebird pair will nest
in a tree hollow.*

predators and scavengers follow them. A few, like the coyote and raven, are as adept in the harsh winters as they are in the fat days of autumn.

On a sage and bitterbrush hillside a female coyote emerges from the steep entrance to her den as the whimper of her hungry pups drifts out of the burrow. Moving quickly away in the direction of a lodgepole forest, the coyote trots quietly down a game trail. Stopping often to listen and test the wind for prey, she reaches the river, where she works slowly through deep grass and dried sedge and finds a few mice and voles. She turns downstream toward the scant remains of a winter-killed elk lying on the gravel bank. Magpies flutter away at her approach and scold her from nearby willow limbs. The bones are scattered and picked clean, but the coyote gnaws briefly on a piece of tough elk hide. She continues downstream, finding only a few small rodents, but nothing large enough to feed her pups. When she discovers the bony remains of a fish, she is watched by a bald eagle that dropped them from its perch high overhead. In a huge stick nest on the limbs of a cottonwood tree, the eagle's mate sits incubating eggs.

The coyote bursts from the cover of riverside willows in pursuit of a pair of Canada Geese preening on the shore, but the wary pair launch themselves out into the water. They paddle noisily across the river channel and climb onto a small island, where they continue to honk at the intruder. The coyote inspects the bank for a nest or a stray gosling but the goose nest is safely hidden in the tangle of a driftwood pile on another island. The coyote hunts on.

She cuts through a stand of dense blue spruce and out into a marshy field of sedge and willow. She circles a cow moose at a distance and pauses only long enough to sniff for a hidden calf. Crossing a beaver dam, she moves up onto an aspen-covered hillside. Here she stops suddenly and turns into the breeze. The odor of deer comes to her, and she quickly picks her way through the underbrush to find a flock of ravens feeding on an old mule deer that has succumbed to the accumulated stress of winter. She scatters the ravens with a charge and circles the carcass, then begins to tear at the meat.

By the time the first snow blankets the high country, the coyotes will be yipping and barking across the cold valleys. Flocks of waxwings, lingering to feed on late ripening berries, will sift through stands of mountain ash trees. The weasel and snowshoe hare will have turned white, and the great bears gone to their winter sleep. The coyote's thick fur will protect her, and her keen nose will find food through the long winter months. Mice will be found buried deep under snow in the meadows, and a few straggling waterfowl will be caught near the frozen shore. More of the weakest deer and elk will fall, and so the coyotes and ravens will feast.

Water lilies cover a shallow
pond in northern Montana.
As glaciers of the Ice Age
retreated, they left buried in
the soil many chunks of ice
that eventually melted to
form ponds or potholes.

One of the most colorful
birds of the Rocky Mountain
pine and spruce forests, the
western tanager was first
described by Lewis and
Clark on their exploration
of the West.

*An unsuspecting salmon is
pulled from its spawning
bed by a bald eagle. Thousands of fish gathering in
shallow headwaters to lay
their eggs attract predators
like the bald eagle.*

*November snow dusts
a spruce tree and the
numerous bald eagles
perched on its limbs. When
the spawning salmon are
gone, the eagles will
continue their migration to
their wintering areas.*

*PRECEDING PAGES
A flock of Bohemian and
cedar waxwings descends
on a berry-laden mountain
ash tree. The nutritious
berries are a favorite of
waxwings, which nest late to
harvest the ripe berries for
their fledging young.*

BALD EAGLE
notes from the field

Kokanee are a landlocked race of sockeye salmon that inhabit Flathead Lake in western Montana. For many years great numbers of these kokanee would migrate during their fall spawning season up into the streams that empty into Flathead Lake. Here they would find the shallow water where they had hatched and lay their own eggs. Although the fish population is currently low from environmental disturbance or natural cyclic conditions, at one time their numbers were great. One of the streams where the salmon spawned is McDonald Creek in Glacier National Park, a slow-moving, meandering stream that drains Lake McDonald in the west end of the park.

McDonald Creek winds back and forth across the flat floor of the steep-sided valley. The side hills are covered with dense stands of tamarack and spruce, and the valley floor is covered with willows and scattered, tall spruce trees.

From late October to late November, McDonald Creek was full of salmon, and the annual event had attracted many wild animals that came to catch and feed on the fish. The most numerous and conspicuous to congregate here was the bald eagle, with 400 to 600 of the raptors in the narrow valley during peak years. They would spend the day perched in trees along the river, swooping down to catch salmon and carrying them to a snag to feed. On an average day each eagle would catch and eat half a dozen fish. At sundown the eagles would fly across Lake McDonald to roost in a grove of cottonwoods. When the spawning ended the eagles would continue on their migration.

I spent each day from daylight to dusk on a bridge that crossed the creek, watching and photographing the eagles. I began to focus my attention on their favorite perches and fishing spots, and I learned their daily cycles of feeding and resting. If the temperature was twenty to thirty degrees below zero, the eagles would stay perched all day. On those days I would watch the banks of the creek to find other animals attracted to the bounty. Coyotes would sneak out to grab salmon splashing near shore, and grizzlies would leave their tracks in the snow where they came at night to eat fish. Even white-tailed deer waded out to eat an occasional salmon.

A bald eagle in Glacier Park sits in a wash of yellow tamarack trees on a hillside overlooking its fishing streams. Tamaracks have deciduous needles that turn color and drop off in the fall just as leaves do.

In the last light of the day, a mature bald eagle glides from its perch in the shadows toward a fish it has spotted in the stream below.

notes from the field *(continued)*

The eagles found a huge, lone spruce perfect for sitting and watching for salmon. They would glide down from the tree to catch fish in an eddy in the creek. By carefully watching the eagles I was able to capture them on film just as they grabbed the salmon.

One of my favorite images was of a mature female eagle that the park biologists had reported sighting for several years. She had only one foot, the other probably lost to a muskrat trap. She would show up in late November. I began watching her because she was bolder than the other eagles and would fly low over the bridge to her perch upstream. Like clockwork she would return two hours later to catch another fish. I set up and waited. When she returned to fish it was efficient and quick; she flew downriver really low, grabbed the first salmon she had a chance for, and went back to her perch, I framed my composition where there was a shaft of sunlight coming through the surrounding ridges and shining on the river. I predetermined the exposure for a white head and tail in sunlight, and when she flew downstream toward me I exposed a series of frames of her in flight. The background was a jumble of trees in deep shade and nearly four *f*-stops darker than the bird's white feathers. One frame caught her against an expecially dense stand of trees that came through as black on the film.

It is unfortunate this large gathering of eagles no longer occurs in the Flathead valley, for it was one of the most spectacular scenes in nature. Perhaps someday the salmon will return and the eagles will again find their way to the valley.

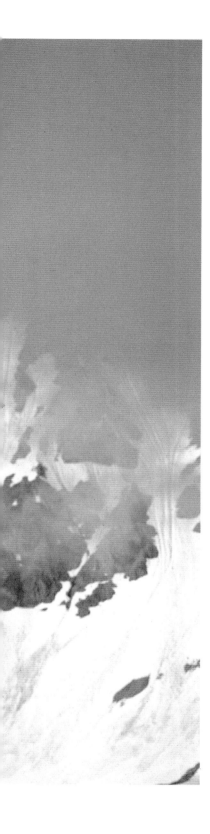

The slopes of a glacier-
scarred mountain form a
cold backdrop for a bald
eagle soaring in spring
winds. From this height, the
eagle can spot fish or other
eagles feeding many miles
away in the narrow valley.

A pair of bald eagles arrives
at their nesting territory in
early spring to begin courtship. They return each year
to the same nest, adding
sticks until it may be as
much as eight feet in width.

PRECEDING PAGES
After their nesting duties
are completed, a pair of
bald eagles sits together in a
cottonwood tree near their
territory. Their young, dark
brown and without the
characteristic white head
and tail, are often mistaken
for golden eagles. Their
white plumage appears
when they reach the age of
four.

A pair of kestrels, the smallest falcon in North America, rests between bouts of courtship and of defense of their nest site. The blue-tinted male will defend the site while the female finds a suitable hollow.

Aspen trees stand dormant through the cold months of winter. Reproducing by sending up new shoots from horizontal roots, aspens may form long rows across a meadow as their roots parallel a stream.

*An alert moose calf stands
close to its protective mother.
Different races of moose
throughout the continent
vary in size, and all can
act unpredictably when
guarding their young.*

*A small cousin of the
grizzly, the black bear is
found throughout the
United States in forested
mountains. Its color ranges
from black to cinnamon to
nearly white. Unlike the
grizzly, the black bear is
skilled at climbing trees.*

Rooted deep in the bottom
of a beaver pond, a water-
lily floats its leaves on the
surface. Fish often hide in
the shade of the large, flat
pads.

A trumpeter swan incubates
its eggs in a nest of rushes.
The swans mate for life and
return each year to the
same site to rebuild their
nest, often on a beaver
lodge or muskrat house.

FOLLOWING PAGES
A cow elk crosses the
Yellowstone River in the
fog created by the cold
morning air and the river's
warm water.

*Yellowstone's first winter
storm mantles a bull elk
and his harem in the
meadow where they nap.
As the mating season ends
and snows deepen, the elk
will move to lower valleys
and open hillsides.*

*Sunrise reveals a cow elk
seeking out fresh green
shoots on the banks of the
Yellowstone River.*

ELK AND COYOTE
notes from the field

At the end of October, Yellowstone Park was about to close for the winter. It had snowed sixteen inches in three days and the entire park had suddenly become quiet, as if the animal life were waiting to see if this was the arrival of deepest winter.

I found a small band of elk in a very serene setting. It was the end of the mating season, and a large bull had his harem of cows and calves bedded down in a sheltered meadow. The weather was extremely variable—snowing hard one minute, sunny the next. When I found the herd of elk, they were coated with a blanket of fresh snow where they lay in the meadow, and the sun was breaking through the storm with a clean, soft light. I had taken a few photographs of the elk bedded down when the bull got up to bugle an answer to another bull off in the timber a half-mile away. Their challenges echoed through the meadow, then the snowfall returned, and the meadow became quiet again.

That afternoon I saw a coyote cross the road ahead of me as I was leaving the park. She had beautiful, thick fur and looked ready for winter. As she started to hunt for mice I followed along on foot. She obviously knew I was no threat to her, and would ignore me as long as I kept my distance. I stayed with her for several hours, catching her in different poses as she hunted along the edges of the lodgepole pine forest and through steamy thermal areas. By the time it started getting dark, I had shot six rolls of film. When I turned to go back to the car I realized that I had been so intent on the coyote that I wasn't sure which direction to go. I had to follow our tracks back to the road and in doing that I came to appreciate how many miles a coyote covers in its zigzag course to find food.

Oblivious to the stark beauty of Yellowstone's thermal formations, a small band of elk crosses the terraces of Mammoth Hot Springs in search of forage. Elk winter where the warm ground keeps snow from accumulating.

Her thick winter fur will protect this female coyote in the sub-zero temperatures of the months ahead, and her keen hearing and sense of smell will enable her to locate rodents living under the snow.

Among the most adaptable
and persistent mountain
predators are the coyotes.
The valleys often echo at
night with their howling and
yelping chorus.

Originally a plains animal,
the elk has retreated to high
mountain meadows and
forests. As the first snow
arrives, this bull elk bugles
a challenge to rivals for
control of his harem of
cows.

FOLLOWING PAGES
Ice on a Yukon lake slowly
recedes with the arrival of
spring. The colors of the
sunset last for hours as the
season of continual
daylight approaches.

A greater sandhill crane
leads its chick toward the
grass where it will find its
first meal of insects.

A three-day-old sandhill
crane colt stands in a bed
of lupine. Within two
months, the young crane
will have grown to be nearly
four feet tall.

*With its incredibly sharp
eyesight and hearing, the
great gray owl locates mice
in the grass below its perch.
These owls hunt in the
morning and evening and
in more northern forests
during the day.*

*The forest-dwelling great
gray owl, the largest of
North American owls,
locates its prey with its
facial disc of feathers acting
as a parabolic reflector that
gathers and pinpoints
sound.*

GREAT GRAY OWL
notes from the field

I hear stories from people who come into my photography gallery about wildlife they have seen. Different visitors were relaying reports to me of a great gray owl observed catching mice in a particular meadow near the Snake River. By the fourth report, I realized there must be a nesting pair of owls that hunted there regularly.

I went out for six evenings and sat on a hillside above the meadow and watched until dusk. The meadow was in a clearing at the edge of the river bottom where a thick blue spruce forest grew, and each day just at dusk one of the owls would fly out of the forest to land in a few scattered aspen trees to hunt for mice and voles. Great gray owls are typically not shy, and by the third day they were accustomed to seeing me. I would move slowly and never approach them directly, and they began to ignore me. It was a very peaceful and silent arrangement in the meadow, with the lengthening shadows and the silent flight of the owls in the calm air.

With his antlers gathering snow, a bull moose naps in the river-bottom land where he winters. His long legs enable him to travel through deep snow to feed on the shoots and buds of willows.

One resident of the boreal forest who remains throughout the year is the great gray owl, but in especially hard, snowy winters, the owls will migrate south to the limits of their forests.

FOLLOWING PAGES
The first heavy snowfall of winter blankets a bull moose in his willow-thicket home.

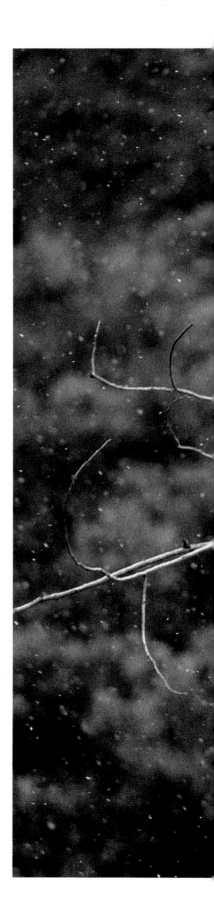

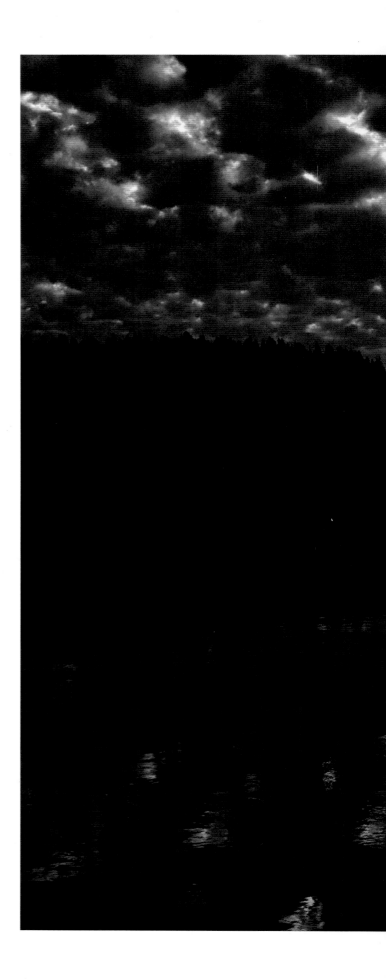

Perched in an alder over-looking a beaver pond, a belted kingfisher watches until the moment when it will dive underwater to grab a fish in its powerful bill.

Cloud patterns of an August sunrise are reflected in a wide bend of the Yellowstone River.

Aspen trees grow on the lower slopes of the Rockies, where their first tinge of autumn color contrasts with surrounding evergreens. They are called "quaking aspens" because their leaves rustle in the slightest breeze.

Fireweed often appears in spectacular blooms that cover meadows and burned or disturbed areas. The tall plants are eaten by deer, elk, and grizzly bears.

Last Mountain Lake at the northern edge of the grass- lands in Saskatchewan is a major staging area for sandhill cranes on their fall migration.

One of the indigenous sounds of the prairies is the flutelike song of the western meadowlark, which nests on the ground but perches on the highest stalks or fence- posts to sing.

GRASSLAND
images of prairie and stream

A dry wind bends the tall grass in waves as it follows the rounded contours of the land, rolling and curling mile after mile. It whistles in the low shrubs, raises dust from exposed hillsides, and sways the tops of trees that grow protected in ravines and along meandering streams. To the north a range of hills breaks the flat plain. In the bottom of a broad valley is a stream that drained away centuries of melting glacier. Tall trees grow along its banks, out of the path of spring floods that carry soil worn from the distant mountains. Animal life is of two kinds: creatures that hide or burrow in the thick mat of grass and roots, and those that move swiftly above it. Low in the southern sky, a flock of sandhill cranes beats slowly into the wind of the last spring snowstorm. The north wind that has swept unimpeded across miles of unbroken land buffets the cranes as they bank sharply and set their wings to descend into the river valley. They glide over cottonwood trees and down into the wide river channel where they pass over ducks and geese to land on a flat sandbar. Over the cranes flies a small flock of pintail ducks in a

A Canada goose wings toward open water where a flock of geese is gathering to migrate.

A Say's phoebe perches momentarily to watch for insects. The phoebe darts and hops almost constantly through grass and brush, feeding on bees, wasps, ants, and flies.

FOLLOWING PAGES
Each evening during spring migration, thousands of sandhill cranes return to roost in the shallow water of the Platte River. During the day, they fly to nearby fields to feed and gain fat reserves for the long flight to nesting grounds in Canada, western Alaska, and Siberia.

courtship flight; they angle back and forth across the river in their display. The cranes roost here for the night, safely surrounded by shallow, flowing water.

At dawn the elegant cranes are moving restlessly. They take off, upstream and into the wind, they circle out of the river bottom and land in a rolling meadow. Here they can watch the miles of open country for predators while they feed on grain and insects. As morning sunlight warms the meadow, pairs of cranes begin to dance, bounding high into the air with their wings half spread and trumpeting their wild call.

On flat ground nearby is a prairie chicken courtship ground, or lek. Here the grassland birds gather at daybreak for their own mating dance. The males display and strut for the females, who watch from the edge of the bare grounds. Soon they will build their nests hidden low in the grass.

When at last warm winds come from the south, the cranes leave their river valley and fly out into the heart of the plains. They traverse vast miles of rolling grassy hills and flat prairie, crossing streams and lakes and pine-filled ravines. They pass over herds of fleet pronghorn antelope in the open country and white-tailed deer in rocky canyons and forested northern hillsides. At night they roost along a prairie pothole, the footprint of a glacier that attracts nesting waterfowl. A coyote watches the cranes land and lopes nearer to investigate, but the tall cranes are wary. The coyote strays off to find easier prey.

Bison, a small remnant of once numberless herds, graze on sweet spring grass in the northern hills. Their red calves start at the sonorous calling of the cranes, but the massive bulls ignore the sound and wander in search of their muddy wallows. The cranes find the shallow water of the glacial potholes too busy and continue on their journey.

Within a few days the sandhill cranes are at the northern end of the grasslands. Soon the open land will give way to thick forests. Here, on the edge of the Canadian prairies where water is plentiful and the gentle land is dotted with lakes and ponds, some of the cranes leave the arctic-bound flock to find nesting sites. One pair returns to their habitual nest on an old beaver lodge in a spring-fed creek; the surrounding water offers protection in the treeless landscape. In the calm morning a male meadowlark sings from a white prairie clover stalk, and the dry clicking of grasshoppers can be heard in the distance. By the time summer's heat arrives and the parched grassland is blackened by sporadic range fires, the fast-growing crane chicks will be wading in the shallows and hiding from predators in willow thickets. As the days grow shorter and a chill comes to the night air, the crane families begin to gather into large flocks. The distant hills are tinged with red and yellow. On a warm Indian summer morning, the calls of distant cranes can be heard to the north; long Vs of cranes and snow geese migrating from the coasts of Alaska and eastern Siberia pass high overhead. The sandhills are eager to join the flocks from the far north, and they rise into the breeze. Seeking out thermal updrafts, they soar in great, spiraling flocks, filling the sky thousands of feet above the prairie. The winds of autumn will carry them south across the plains to their winter home.

When cyclical populations of their prey reach low levels, snowy owls often appear in the farm country of Alberta, Canada, in search of food. A granary built in the 1930s serves as an observation perch.

The powerful snowy owl watches from a fencepost for prey. In the absence of its preferred diet of lemmings, the displaced arctic bird will hunt rabbits and weasels and will even attack animals caught in traps.

SNOWY OWL
notes from the field

Snowy owls are normally found in the arctic tundra, nesting on the treeless ground in moss and lichens. But in severe winters they are driven far south in their search for food and often end up in southern Canada and the northern United States. I was in the wheat-farm country of southeastern Alberta in January, trying to photograph the owls that had migrated there. I saw up to six a day but could not get close enough for the image I wanted. I kept seeing the big white owls sitting on fenceposts or straw bales, but in the flat wheatfields I knew I couldn't get near enough to the skittish birds before they would fly off. Even with the use of a long telephoto lens the image of the owl would be too small unless combined with another interesting element. I visualized how great it would be to see an owl on top of one of the decrepit grain storage sheds, built in the 1930s, that dotted the landscape.

I had just about given up for the day and was driving back toward town when I saw the white shape of an owl sitting on the peak of an old granary a mile from the road. There were only about twenty minutes of light left and the temperature was minus 35 degrees, so I grabbed my camera and started walking quickly out toward the granary. I followed a zigzag course, never going directly toward the owl, and I reached an adjacent granary without scaring the bird. I hid in the granary for several minutes and warmed my camera under my coat, and then I peered out. I could tell from the whitewash of droppings on the granary that the bird perched there often, and I knew it would be reluctant to fly off into the intense cold. I stepped out into the open, and the owl looked directly at me. I assumed it was used to the farmer who visited the granaries, so I pretended to ignore the owl and moved slowly out into the field for a better angle. The owl turned its gaze away from me, and I had time to shoot ten exposures before the light faded.

Lacking powerful talons to hold its prey, the loggerhead shrike, a predatory song-bird, impales its victim securely on a thorn or on barbed wire.

A mixture of foxtail and yarrow bends with a prairie wind. Foxtail bristles may cause blindness or death in grazing animals, while yarrow was used by native Americans as a medicine.

*Migrating tundra swans
prepare for a landing in a
shallow prairie pond.
Previously named whistling
swans, they are marked
with a yellow teardrop
shape on the base of their
black bills.*

*Running along the surface
of the water, the heavy
trumpeter swan uses the
distance to work up a full
wingbeat to lift itself into
the air.*

*PRECEDING PAGES
Tundra swans nest on dry
tundra near water in
Alaska and winter along
both coasts of the United
States. Their long migrations
carry them across the
continent twice a year.*

Some of the last herds of bison have found refuge in the wooded canyons and plateaus of the prairies, where deep snow forces them to move in search of new grazing. Bison use their massive heads to sweep the ground clear of snow.

Canada geese mate for life, and the pairs remain together even as winter covers their northern nesting grounds and they migrate south.

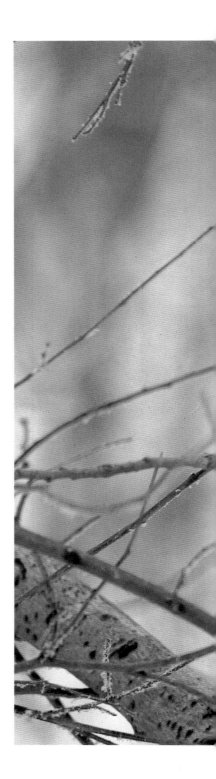

The red-bellied woodpecker lives in thick forest along river bottoms, where it flies from tree to tree to hammer into the wood after insect larvae.

Cardinals live and continue to sing in their brushy home year-round, even in the coldest weather. The males become fiercely territorial in the spring.

Stepping through shallow water in a prairie marsh, an American avocet feeds by sweeping its slender, upcurved bill from side to side as it wades.

A resident of fields and open country, the American goldfinch, sometimes called the thistle bird, feeds on the seeds of grasses, wildflowers, and thistles.

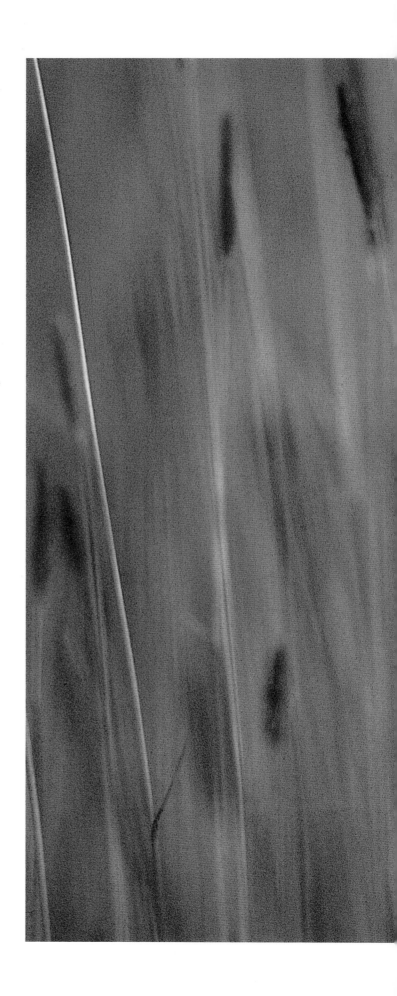

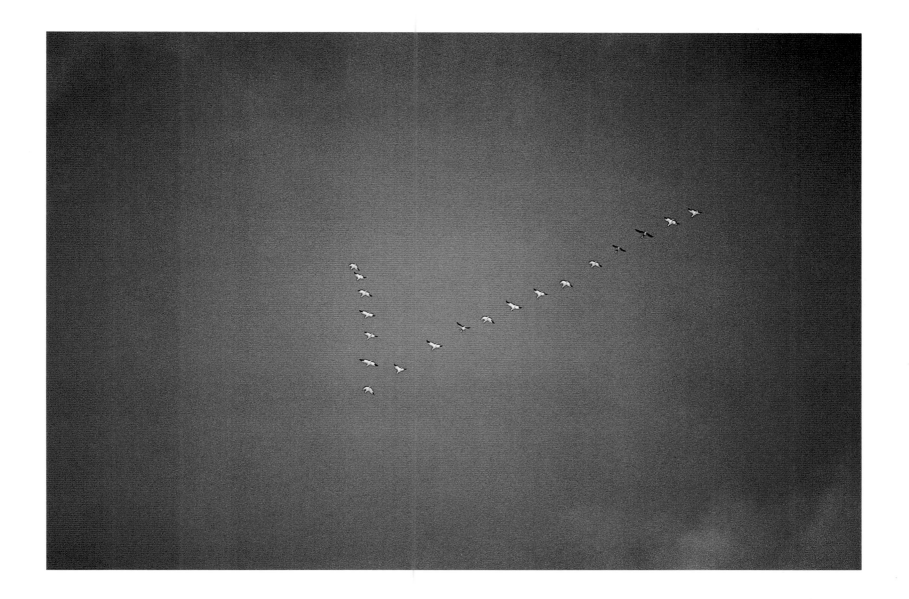

The goldfinch nests late in the season after most other birds have fledged in order to take advantage of the seeds of thistles and other late summer plants.

Huge flocks of up to 200,000 snow geese winter in the river valleys of the southern prairies. The most abundant of wild geese, they nest in large colonies in the arctic tundra.

*With most of their fall
migration behind them, a
flock of snow geese skims
the treetops of a wooded
river bottom.*

*A summer of feeding on
fresh grass has a white-
tailed deer in prime shape
for the fall and winter. A
fleeing buck will flash its
characteristic white tail as
a warning.*

*Found in wooded gullies
and forested bottomland
scattered across the prairies,
the great horned owl, a
large and powerful preda-
tor, hoots a deep call that
carries over considerable
distances in the night.*

*Winter on the prairies finds
a small band of pronghorns
looking for protection from
the wind. As the fastest
North American animal,
and with their sharp vision,
pronghorns are well
adapted to open country.*

FOLLOWING PAGES
*Each year, thousands of
sandhill cranes gather in
staging areas for their long
spring migration to Alaska
and Siberia.*

Canada geese return to their nest island in May to find their pond still frozen and a fresh dusting of snow on the ground. They will defend the island, and the female will build her nest of grass and down.

The Platte River in Nebraska has been used by migrating sandhill cranes for millions of years. Each evening, thousands of cranes return to roost after feeding in surrounding fields and meadows.

PRAIRIE WATERFOWL
notes from the field

My earliest memories are those of the prairies. I remember sitting on the steps of our house in Grand Island, Nebraska, watching my dad come home from hunting with a half-dozen mallards draped around his neck. He would lift the string of heavy drakes over his head and place them at my feet. I was fascinated by their feathers, iridescent green heads, and hard yellowish bills.

My initiation to the prairie world of the Platte River came when I was four. I remember climbing into the brown tin boat filled with the wooden duck and goose decoys Dad had made. On top of the decoys he laid his 12-gauge shotgun and a small army knapsack that contained his duck and goose calls, extra shotgun shells, thermos bottle of coffee, and our lunch of peanut butter sandwiches.

We would leave the south bank of the Platte River in the dark an hour or more before sunrise. So he wouldn't scare any roosting birds, Dad wouldn't use his flashlight once we had started towards the blind, which was a half-mile away through flooded willows and across the open river. He didn't need the light; he had come here every day of the season. At that hour the air was alive with the sounds of ducks and geese moving up and down the river. I could hear the rush of wings and their chattering feed calls overhead and would look up to see only stars in the darkness above. It was an exciting time for me.

Dad's blind consisted of four oaken pickle barrels sunk in the ground on a little willow-covered island in the middle of the channel. Dad had hunted on this island or one nearby since 1932, when he was sixteen. Almost forty years later, my first photographs would be taken from this same blind.

Every day and every year on the river was a new learning experience. The weather more than anything influenced the behavior of the birds and our hunting techniques. Warm, sunny days with south breezes were best for geese, while cold, overcast days with blustery north winds brought the mallards down. When heavy snow blanketed the grain fields of the Dakotas to the north, both ducks and geese would funnel into the Platte. I have vivid memories of those days when we would see flight after flight of migrating waterfowl.

By the end of October most of the pintails, widgeon,

The drake mallard and his less colorful mate are a familiar sight at ponds, creeks, and sloughs, where they feed in shallow water and nest along the shore.

After the nesting season is over, Canada geese gather into flocks for the long flight south.

notes from the field *(continued)*

teal, white-fronted geese and sandhill cranes had already migrated beyond the Platte. In November and December, we saw mostly mallards and Canada geese and small flocks of mergansers, redheads, canvasbacks and goldeneyes.

Dad liked calling geese most of all and taught me how to call them so well that by my high school graduation I won the World's Goose-Calling Championship, a big deal to a boy from Nebraska. But for us, getting high marks from human judges was not nearly as much fun as actually turning a flock of geese and calling them into the decoys.

In March, we witnessed the waterfowl spring migration and the massive flocks of sandhill cranes that staged in the Platte Valley. In June, before the river would nearly go dry, we would go there to catch catfish. In July, my brothers and I would run "naked as jay birds" up and down the river, spearing carp for my grandmother to pickle. I would wade the drying pools to catch stranded minnows, frogs and toads. They would all go home to Mom to join my menagerie of creatures such as crows, raccoons, oppossums, or baby jackrabbits that had been displaced by a farmer's haying operation. Mom was always, or almost always, understanding and willing to take care of my animals. She even kept my nightcrawlers in her refrigerator so I could sell them to my friend the bass fisherman. She wasn't the average mother. In August, we worked on the blind and plowed and cut willows that grew in the dried-up river channels. We tried desperately to keep the encroaching vegetation from taking over the river, which was once "a mile wide and an inch deep." Since the 1930s over 70 percent of the Platte's water has been systematically dammed, diverted, and removed. The river we navigated in the little tin boat is no more.

Except for a traditional hunt with Dad, I haven't hunted in the last ten years, spending most of my time photographing instead. But I will continue to go there with my cameras in the fall to watch for that "bunch of mallards over Lockwood's place" upriver and the wise old flock of Canadas on the "goose highway" to the northeast. I will try to recapture on film the feeling of the Platte River when it was full of water and full of birds and the last of the old-time goose hunters was there with his boy.

Flying in tight formation,
drake pintails courting a
hen race low over the
Platte River.

Although sandhill cranes
forage mostly on dry land,
shallow water is vital for
roosting, and diversion of
shallow grassland rivers
threatens to disrupt their
life cycle.

FOLLOWING PAGES
Shortly before sunrise,
sandhill cranes arrive in a
meadow to feed. One of the
oldest bird species in the
world, crane pairs mate for
life and, in spring, reaffirm
their bond with a courtship
dance on feeding grounds.

*Whooping cranes migrate
in small groups to Wood
Buffalo Park in Canada's
Northwest Territories, where
their only nesting ground
remains.*

*A broad-winged hawk that
soars over open country,
the Swainson's hawk eats
chiefly mice and large
insects. These hawks gather
in tremendous flocks
during their annual fall
migration to South America.*

*Reflections of summer
foliage surround the striking
male wood duck on a creek
near its nest. Wood ducks
nest in tree hollows, often
high off the ground, and
adapt easily to boxes placed
in farm ponds.*

*An iridescent green head
marks the drake mallard,
one of the best-known
ducks.*

Taiga forest and tundra in fall colors surround a lake where a pair of tundra swans feed. The birds nest away from water in the dense mat of moss and grass that covers the arctic ground.

On their way to find fresh grazing, three Dall sheep cross the rock debris of a talus slope in the rugged Alaska range. When winter arrives, the sheep move to lower, windblown hillsides where they can find exposed vegetation.

TUNDRA
images of the north

The spring sun first gleams over the low horizon, and winter begins to lift slowly from the barren regions of the north. Within weeks the rolling tundra and the low ridges begin to warm as the sun arcs higher and longer each day. The mountains that erupt from the smooth landscape will hold their cold snow and ice all year, but on gentle hillsides and rocky outcroppings the increasing heat of the sun melts snow, uncovering lichens and mosses, and life stirs. In a small valley the trickle of water is audible through the last ice and snow covering a stream. Willows begin to emerge from the snow drifts and a gaunt young moose finds new strength in their exposed shoots. Having survived his first winter alone, he slowly works his way several miles downstream toward the broad expanse of a river bottom filled with willow and sedge. The clear spring air is cold, and the first sounds of life carry across the open country. In a wide river basin a small herd of caribou moves up onto the surrounding hillsides. Their long winter diet of lichens and moss has left them thin, and they search

In August and September, when brilliant colors paint the tundra landscape, dwarfed plants that have grown slowly in the brief summer begin their long winter dormancy.

Rising 20,320 feet above sea level, Mount McKinley is the highest peak in North America and dominates the landscape of the range of the caribou. Here a bull wanders his domain during the fall mating season.

hungrily for succulent new growth. Scattered about are the bones of caribou that fell to the harsh wind and extreme arctic temperatures. A cross fox watches the herd for signs of a weak animal, then gnaws patiently on a rib cage and waits.

The herd of caribou grows stronger each day and soon becomes restless. They move out of their valley when the snow melts and follow the contours of the vast country, moving slowly north. The bulls linger behind, leaving the cows and calves until the fall mating season brings them together; they concentrate on finding forage to supply their new antler growth and to gain fat. The herd joins a large group on a traditional migration route, and they move toward their calving grounds and summer range. The mass of caribou grows steadily as more and more herds band together. Driven to follow the trails of their ancestors, they heedlessly cross streams and spread out over the soft tundra.

On an open hillside beneath a rocky outcropping, a grizzly bear digs for ground squirrels under the last patches of snow. Her winter's sleep has burned the fat from her body, and now she must spend the waking season in a relentless search for food. When the scent of the caribou reaches her, she pauses and sniffs the wind, but the breeze changes and she returns to her hunt.

High up on the slopes, where grass and moss begin to give way to bare rock, a small band of Dall sheep pick their way across a talus slope to find forage. Overhead, the first flocks of migrating cranes pass by on their way to the far north.

At last, the caribou reach their calving grounds. Soon, newborn calves are nursing and scampering through the scattered herd. Wolves find the caribou and prey on the weak and careless, and scavenging foxes and birds clean the bones. When the calves are strong the herd moves on to their summering range, where they will fatten on the year's rich growth.

Here the ground beneath them is permanently frozen, and the melting water of winter forms ponds, sloughs and marshes on the tundra. Thousands of waterfowl find their way to nest here, where their young can feed and grow in continual daylight. In the distance, an arctic loon calls from the lake where it nests.

Far to the north, beyond the end of the tundra and out onto the ice, the great polar bear reigns.

The autumnal arctic sun begins to drop toward the horizon as fast as it climbed in the spring, and soon the caribou are on the move again. From summer vegetation their diet reverts back to moss and lichens. The heavy-antlered bulls challenge each other for the right to breed. By the time the mating is over, the caribou are moving across frozen ground to their wintering range. They break up into smaller bands. Soon they will be back on windswept, treeless hillsides, pawing through snow to find food.

Scavenging for scraps left by predators, a magpie watches a red fox from a respectful distance.

On their way to wintering grounds, caribou head across the foothills of the Alaska Range. Herds travel much of the year, to summer and winter ranges, to calving grounds, and in search of forage.

On the ornately symmetrical antlers of the caribou, a velvet covering supplies blood for antler growth. This dries when the antlers mature and is rubbed off by the time of the fall mating season.

Leaving its winter range, a bull caribou seeks out fresh green vegetation to supply the nutrients needed for antler growth.

Wind and cold limit the growth of trees along the Hudson Bay, home to the polar bear. Farther to the north, there lies only flat tundra and ice.

Each fall, polar bears leave the tundra and hunt seals on the ice of the Hudson Bay. A plodding gait is the most energy efficient speed for the massive bears, who quickly overheat when running.

PRECEDING PAGES
Walking beside the huge tracks of another bear, a polar bear heads out onto the ice. The bear's broad feet help distribute its weight on the ice and function as paddles in water.

POLAR BEAR
notes from the field

It was the afternoon of the first day of November. From the airplane window I could see the tracks of a lone polar bear in the fresh snow below, heading east in a nearly straight line toward the Hudson Bay. Ten minutes later we landed on the small airstrip at Churchill, Manitoba. I had left Wyoming and its Indian summer the day before, and now found myself in what looked and felt like deepest winter of January.

Home to the most successful population of polar bears, Churchill and nearby Hudson Bay is an area I had wanted to visit for many years. To see the great white bear crossing the snowy, icy tundra would be a dream come true. I couldn't wait for the plane to be unloaded so I could get out of town in hopes of seeing a bear. This far north the days of November are fairly short, and by the time we sorted out our gear and drove to the outskirts of town the daylight was nearly gone. From a bluff overlooking the bay we watched the sun dip below the horizon as a pair of ravens rode the wind along the frozen shoreline. The light in the arctic is special—perhaps because of the crisp, clean air, perhaps because of the low angle of the sun. I envisioned the golden yellow bears in this kind of light, but we would not see the sun again for five days.

Late that evening we drove out to the research station, and when we were far from the town's lights we saw the aurora borealis lighting up a cloud bank to the north. Returning to Churchill after midnight, we saw a pretty red fox in the headlights as it crossed the icy road in front of us. It is difficult for me to sleep on nights like this, anticipating the day to come, and I awakened to the sound of the wind very early in the morning. When it became light I could see sheets of snow blowing across the window; weather conditions change suddenly and unpredictably here. My companions were none too happy about the change in weather, but I had come here for images of bears in all kinds of weather conditions and I had to forget about the wonderful arctic light of the evening before. A major blizzard seemed perfect—the bears would appear ghostlike in blowing snow and I thought it would be a great arctic setting. However, the blizzard was so "perfect" that even the four-wheel drive tundra buggies that sit high

While waiting for Hudson Bay waters to freeze, the normally solitary polar bears find time to socialize.

A polar bear sleeps in a low spot out of the wind. During their waiting period by the Hudson Bay, the bears live mostly on their fat reserves and are inactive much of the day.

notes from the field *(continued)*

off the ground on six-foot tractor tires couldn't leave town because of the drifting snow and poor visibility. That afternoon the wind and snow subsided and we were able to drive out to the bay twenty miles east of town.

The great number of species that come here to nest in the summer, such as snow geese and various shorebirds, had gone south; the land was quiet except for the occasional raucous call of a raven. Only a small number of hardy species remained—arctic foxes that scavenged the remains of the seals killed by the bears, snowy owls, ptarmigan, and a few ivory gulls and gyrfalcons.

As we drove to the bay I spotted a large adult bear at some distance, traveling into the wind with head and neck outstretched, as if following a scent. There was only snow and a bit of yellow grass bending in the wind, the yellow-tinged white bear, and a dark, somber sky on the horizon. It was the scene I had come here for.

Soon we saw a younger, grayish-white bear sleeping in the open just off the road near a small stump. It ignored us as we drove by, barely opening its eyes—polar bears are rarely threatened by anything except a larger bear. Since anything or anyone on foot is a potential meal for a bear, most photography is done from the safety of either a vehicle or from a semi-permanent tundra buggy camp. The bears rarely pay any attention except when lunch is being served or dinner is being cooked. The curious bears would sometimes follow the scent of food to our camp, then stand on their hind legs and brace themselves with their huge front paws against the side of the camp's dining car. They could look in the windows with penetrating eyes or smell with their wet, black noses what was being served. Looking eye-to-eye with a polar bear standing ten feet tall and only a few feet away is unforgettable!

It is difficult to describe the feeling of seeing a polar bear in its natural environment, perhaps because to me polar bears are so symbolic. Like the wolf, the loon, the whooping crane, and the grizzly bear, they are survivors in a world that at best has only tolerated their existence. In the face of that treatment they still represent the best of what I feel to be truly wild.

Cold arctic water is an essential element of the polar bear's habitat. Skilled swimmers, polar bears have been observed stalking seals by swimming under the ice and emerging to surprise the seal.

Although the cubs are nearly pure white, polar bears develop a yellowish tinge and are often stained by the fat of seals. Since their prey is available all year, there is no need for these huge carnivores to hibernate.

An arctic fox follows the trail of a polar bear across the ice. Foxes scavenge the remains of seals left behind by the bears.

FOLLOWING PAGES
With its well-insulated body and bulky legs and feet, no other animal is as well suited to live in the harsh world of the arctic as the polar bear. Males may weigh 1,500 pounds and measure ten feet from nose to tail.

Willow ptarmigan in mottled late-summer plumage blend into the surrounding tundra vegetation. In winter, the birds are pure white.

A beaver in an Alaskan pond spends the brief summer and fall cutting and storing willow shoots for the winter. The branches are anchored in the mud of the bottom and used when the pond freezes over.

FOLLOWING PAGES
A bull moose stands silhouetted against an arctic sunset. When snow begins to fall, the moose will travel to lower elevations and spend the winter where it can feed on willow buds and twigs.

A pika pauses briefly from its busy routine of cutting and storing grass for the winter. By the time snow covers its rocky home, the pika will have dried and stored enough food in its "haystacks" to last through the winter.

Although its place in a structured and regulated world is a matter of controversy, no one can deny that the wolf is a beautiful and inspiring animal worth the effort of preservation.

*Two Dall sheep, the only
wild white sheep in the
world, rest on a hillside in
the mountains of Alaska.*

*Near the end of the Dall
sheep's rutting season, a
ram beds down where he
can watch a ewe in the
rocks below. Dall sheep must
find an exposed ridge or
hillside in winter so they
can paw through the snow
for vegetation, and they
depend on cold winters to
keep the snow light
and powdery.*

*FOLLOWING PAGES
Winter nights on the tundra
are often spectacularly lit
up by the aurora borealis,
or northern lights. Electrical
disturbances in the upper
atmosphere cause the effect.*

The grizzly bear's claws are used for digging roots, insect grubs, and rodents from the ground, and here, for delicately holding a branch while it eats soapberries.

Even a massive grizzly bear is dwarfed by its immense tundra domain. An omnivorous animal, it feeds on plants, especially berries and tubers, much of the spring and summer.

GRIZZLY BEAR
notes from the field

I was in Denali Park, Alaska, trying for photographs of grizzly bears. It was fall, and the animals were making preparations for winter, trying to put on fat for the coming lean months of sleep. Nearly every day for a month my friend Dan Fulton and I observed one particular sow with a cub digging arctic ground squirrels from their burrows in the tundra. The parka squirrels, as they are sometimes called, were also preparing for hibernation and were very fat.

This sow had a larger than normal appetite for squirrels. Once she had seen, heard, or smelled one, she would do anything to catch it. The squirrels would almost always see her first, give out a warning bark and scurry into their burrows, which normally have multiple tunnels and exits. First the sow would try to pinpoint the exact location of the squirrel by sniffing and listening. Then she would stand on her hind legs and drop with her front paws on top of the likely hiding place—a sort of shock wave approach. She would repeat the tactic several times, hoping to scare the rodent from its burrow. If this failed, she would start digging. Then it would be only a matter of time.

To see a 400-pound bear digging up a one-pound ground squirrel was more impressive than I would have imagined. Sometimes she would tear up an area the size of a living room. Willows and dwarf birch and their root systems would be completely ripped out of the tundra, and all we would see was the bear's brown rump sticking up out of the giant hole. Her cub would lie down nearby to watch and wait, sometimes twenty minutes or more. The sow's expenditure of energy for the energy she would obtain seemed pretty inefficient, but the fresh protein was apparently worth it.

It was always interesting to watch this behavior, but it generally took place in heavy willows or too far away to photograph. At the last second, when the rodent would try to flee, the bear would pin it to the ground before it got out of the torn-up burrow. Dan and I talked about how great it would be to see this close up, but we make a practice of never approaching grizzly bears on foot. We hoped to see her one day near the road and watch from the safety of our vehicle.

Amid stunted arctic vegetation, a grizzly bear continues its summer-long search for food to fatten it for the coming winter sleep. The light color of the tips of its hairs creates the grizzled effect that gives the bear its name.

An arctic ground squirrel flees a surprisingly agile grizzly. The persistent bear eventually excavates enough of the rodents to give it a portion of the valuable protein it needs for hibernation.

notes from the field *(continued)*

One day after a fresh snowfall, we were driving through the park and saw the sow and her cub running down a creek bed toward us. When she was about 75 yards away, she turned and ran up the willow-covered bank. We recognized her and her "squirrel routine." We jumped out of the car and set up the tripod and camera with the 600-mm lens. Although we could barely see her thrashing around in the willows, she remained close to the open creek bed, so we figured there was a chance that a squirrel might sneak out of the willows and make a break for it. We weren't set up for more than ten seconds when it happened. The squirrel was running madly across the snow 25 yards from the bear. When she realized the squirrel was no longer under foot, she stood up, spotted the racing squirrel, and went immediately in pursuit. The little rodent tried to out-maneuver the massive bear by running a figure-eight pattern. Until that moment I had never realized the power and the quickness of a determined grizzly bear. As the squirrel made a sharp left turn, the bear closed in, and I heard my last frame of film go through the camera. My mind raced, wondering if I had actually captured the most impressive animal behavior I had ever seen. Had I run out of film one frame too soon?

A bull moose stands ready to defend his ground during the fall rutting season. By the time the rut is over, he may have a harem of fifteen or twenty cows.

Shallow arctic lakes are ideal for moose to wade in search of aquatic vegetation. Mount McKinley looms in the background.

FOLLOWING PAGES
Twilight silhouettes a bull caribou on a ridge over-looking his tundra summer range. After the fall rutting season, the bulls begin to lose their antlers and, by January, most will have dropped them.

The call of loons from an Alaskan lake echoes over the tundra. Most of the world's wilderness areas are now in the cold, remote north country where the loons nest.

The arctic loon raises its young on the shallow, fresh-water lakes of the tundra. At the end of the summer, the young migrate with their parents to winter along salt-water coasts.

*As the changing colors of
tundra vegetation testify,
the arctic summer is coming
to an end for this tiny wood
frog.*

*Winter temperatures and
scarcity of food take their
toll on the herds of caribou.
The winter-killed animals
are scavenged by foxes,
ravens, and grizzlies in
the spring.*

Sunrise near Buffalo Springs, Kenya, accentuates the shape of an acacia tree. Nocturnal predators find their day beds as the sky brightens and the plains come to life.

A pair of white-throated bee eaters watches for bees and wasps to fly near. The birds fly off their perch to pluck their prey from the air, then return to their perch and repeatedly knock the bee against a limb until it discharges all its venom.

ANCIENT PLAINS
images of Africa

. . . .

An African landscape slowly takes shape in the dim light of early morning. The first hint of sunrise on the distant horizon reveals an outline of worn and rounded hills and, beyond that, the massive, ancient volcanic mountains. As the sky grows light, details of the Serengeti plain begin to show. The crowns of thorny acacia trees are silhouetted against the sunrise, and egrets and cranes roosting in the trees stretch their wings and look for signs of movement out on the grassy plains. The barking of jackals from a dry riverbed mixes with the chorus of bird life awakening in the forest. Within minutes every detail of the immense landscape is unveiled in the clear morning air. The rich, green grass that stretches smoothly to the mountainous horizon is broken by scattered stands of trees and herd after herd of grazing animals. The sky is as vast as the land; to the east it begins to fill with billowy cumulus clouds. Sky, grassland, and animals seem to flow in parallel planes from horizon to horizon as the first morning breeze stirs. The clouds drift, the life-giving grass sways, and gazelle and wildebeest

. . . .

*Able to survive on scaveng-
ing alone, a white-backed
vulture glides in for a
landing. With their sharp
eyesight and countless hours
of soaring on thermal
currents, vultures are
usually the first to locate
animals killed by predators
such as lions or leopards.*

*A group of giraffes stands
where they blend into the
pattern of trees in Masai
Mara, Kenya. The giraffes
use their prehensile upper
lip and tongue to pull
foliage from high limbs.*

herds begin to seek out water.

By late afternoon, intense sunlight washes over the grassland, drying the mud at the edge of a waterhole where a pair of elegant giraffes has come to drink. Impalas, fleeing the waves of heat, move to the scant shade of the acacias. Across the expanse of open country a thin haze of dust rises into the air. The giraffes leave their waterhole and stride off toward a line of acacias to feed off the high foliage. A cattle egret follows in their wake to find prey in the tall grass they disturb with their feet.

As shadows from the mountains creep across open country toward the forest, wildebeest and zebras find their places for the night, bunching together in the open or seeking thick brush near the trees. Hyenas discover a wildebeest cow with her calf separated from the herd and move in for an opportunity to attack. In low tree limbs along the forest edge, a pair of white-throated bee eaters and a paradise flycatcher dart from their perches after insects awakened by the coolness of the evening.

From a tree, where it can see much of the surrounding country, a leopard watches lazily as the sun sinks behind the rolling hills. At a jumble of rocks and shrubs, lions spend their days in the shade and cubs wrestle and wait for the females to make a kill. The huge males lie sleeping in the grass and occasionally raise their heads to test the breeze. Farther out into the plain is an old termite mound where the cheetah and her cubs sit and watch the gazelle herd. She waits for one gazelle to come close, stalks out into the grass, then makes her final, incredible burst of speed.

The leopard prefers to wait until darkness comes to slip into the forest to make a kill. But now it sees a young impala wander off from its herd and feed under the spreading limbs of a nearby tree. The leopard tenses its muscles in anticipation of a stalk, then slips stealthily out of the tree and onto the ground. It crouches low in the grass, then begins to move slowly forward, its spotted coat blending almost perfectly with the vegetation. Inch by inch it creeps closer to the impala. Just as the leopard hunches down to spring from the grass, a cry of alarm from a spurfowl startles the impala fawn. The leopard reacts and bursts from cover to grab the fawn as it turns and stumbles. The leopard feeds on the kill then drags it back up into the tree where jackals and vultures cannot reach it.

Night falls, and the leopard leaves its kill and drops down to prowl the edge of the forest. It hears the hyenas who are after the wildebeest calf and the deep roar of a lion in the distance. The leopard returns to its tree limb at daybreak and lets its kill fall to scavengers on the ground. On the plain the lions have made a kill, and jackals surround and cover a shape near a waterhole. Each night the immense herds are minutely reduced, but each day brings new births. Now the morning sun reaches into the leopard's tree to color the mixed patterns of animal and leaf, and the leopard sleeps.

Although the leopard hunts mostly in the forest at night, the spotted pattern of its coat makes it nearly invisible to other animals when it stalks in the grass during the day.

A leopard watches the movements of a herd of gazelles. If successful in a kill, it will drag its prey into the tree where scavengers cannot reach it.

As the sun sets over Masai Mara, Kenya, a leopard awakens to the sounds and smells of evening. When darkness falls, the leopard will move silently into nearby forest to hunt.

One of the more spectacular birds of the African plains, a crowned crane is unmistakable with its straw-colored crest of bristle-like feathers.

An anubis baboon is alert to predators in the Ngorongoro Crater. Baboons are mostly terrestrial and live on rocks and hillsides in the open country.

On a forested hillside surrounding the flat crater floor, a glory lily blooms in the warmth of Ngorongoro Crater.

Elephants are highly social, and the herd reacts quickly to surround a calf separated from its mother. Although the adult elephant has no predator other than humans, calves can be taken by lions.

Elephants cross the Ngorongoro Crater floor. Because of their tremendous appetites and need for water, elephants move constantly to find adequate nourishment—as much as a quarter of a ton a day.

PRECEDING PAGES
Elephants in Amboseli National Park raise clouds of dust in the late afternoon sun. A marshy spot nearby supplies the herd with water.

ELEPHANTS
notes from the field

. . . .

A pair of giraffes crossed the rough, dusty road in front of us. Beyond them, through the haze of mid-day, we could see Kilimanjaro 75 miles away across the Kenyan border in Tanzania. Beyond the arid bush country, the short-grass plains opened up and we started seeing small herds of zebra and Thomson's gazelles. By late afternoon we had reached the thick green oasis at the heart of Amboseli National Park, a relatively small area surrounded by sunbaked mud, with dust devils whirling around its perimeter.

As we drove down a small track through the center of the grassy carpet we saw many different birds: black-headed herons, royal spoonbills, jacanas, crowned plovers, and a sacred ibis. We stopped to watch a herd of cape buffalo cross a marshy area. A flock of cattle egrets followed along, several catching rides on the backs of the buffalo.

When we turned to the west there was an incredible sight—about 150 elephants of all sizes were feeding, drinking, and bathing. They were in family groups, each led by a matriarch. We stopped the car and watched and waited. New family groups had come from the hot, dry plains to get water. We were soon surrounded by the herd, some passing within a few feet of our vehicle. We tried to remain quiet and hoped nothing would disturb them. One young calf got separated from its mother and started squealing and trumpeting and racing through the shallow marsh from one family group to another. Soon others started trumpeting and flapping their giant ears in response. Although it seemed longer, it was probably only a few minutes before a large female walked out of a family group and went over to the calf, laid her trunk across the calf's shoulders, and urged it toward the edge of the water. Here the herd was mud-bathing, trying to stay cool and keep away the biting insects. After satisfying their thirst and squirting great quantities of water and mud on themselves, they headed across the open flats. We watched the sun set and photographed their ghostly silhouettes as they headed towards the yellow-fever trees where they would spend the night.

The following morning we returned to the same area hoping to get some images of elephants with the sun rising

. . . .

A cow elephant rests in the shade during the heat of the day in Amboseli.

Bull elephants face off. Although the herd is led by an old female, and most of the interaction of males is nonviolent sparring, the bulls may fight for the right to breed. Older bulls will separate from the herd and live in solitude.

notes from the field *(continued)*

on Kilimanjaro. But shortly after daybreak, clouds gathered and obscured the mountain. Only fifteen elephants had returned to the area with a half-dozen cattle egrets searching for insects around the moving elephant feet.

We drove farther west and followed a lioness as she crossed a dry lake bed and marked the edges of her territory with her scent. In a small marsh, we watched a malachite kingfisher hunt from papyrus grass and, beyond the marsh, a huge, lone bull elephant with great ivory tusks moving toward the hill country to the south. I wondered how a bull of this size and age had survived the poachers. He disappeared down a brushy, overgrown riverbed.

With hopes of getting another glimpse of him, we followed the track along the escarpment. A mile or so along the narrow, winding road we flushed a few vultures out of the dense bush. There, thirty yards off the track was a huge mound covered with dirt and brush. Four legs and a faceless elephant head stuck out from the debris. The tusks were gone. Flies covered the body, and vultures waited nearby. The twenty-five-year-old female elephant, named Jennifer, had been killed the day before. Joyce Poole, one of the elephant researchers in Amboseli, said that the female was one of her favorites, which she had observed for many years. It was yet another senseless killing in a long list of elephants she had gotten to know.

Of all the large and exotic mammals on the continent, the elephant seems the least able to tolerate its predicament in the modern world. On the same path of extermination as the black rhino, it has never been more threatened than today. Because of huge profit in the ivory trade and widespread corruption it is almost impossible to stop the poaching. Fully a third of all illegal elephant ivory ends up in the United States. Unless we want to be satisfied with a token population of elephants in zoos and circuses, we should do everything possible to ban and boycott all ivory products. It is the elephant's last chance.

During our last evening in Amboseli we watched a small herd of wildebeest frolicking on a dusty hillside. In the distance, silhouetted against a beautiful African sunset, two young bull elephants were sparring. It was difficult to imagine a different Africa—one without elephants. As we drove away into the growing darkness, I wished them well.

The unadaptable black
rhinoceros has been all but
eliminated from its natural
range in Africa by horn
poachers. Red-billed
oxpeckers feed on insects
and parasites attracted to
the rhinoceros.

A pair of crowned cranes
flies to a new feeding
ground in Ngorongoro
Crater.

FOLLOWING PAGES

*When the rains come to
Masai Mara, they bring the
promise of a new season of
the plant growth so vital to
the impala, one of the
fleetest animals of the
plains. When frightened
or chased, the herd makes
an incredible, leaping,
zigzagging escape.*

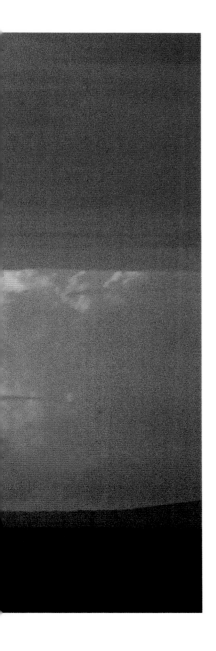

Lightning is soon to cross the skies as the heat of late afternoon generates spectacular thunder clouds over the Serengeti plains.

Soon after sunrise, female impalas stand alert at the forest's edge. These delicate animals can cover thirty feet in their running leaps.

*Wildebeest charge playfully
in dusty Amboseli. Also
called gnu, they gather near
a waterhole in dry weather
and may migrate by the
tens of thousands in search
of forage and water.*

Nothing else so epitomizes the African grasslands as the shaggy mane and head of the male lion. Because lions expend twice the energy as other animals do to move, the powerful males spend the heat of the day sleeping and resting in the grass.

A cattle egret hitches a ride on the back of a cape buffalo. The egret follows the buffalo through the grass and catches insects disturbed by the buffalo's feet.

A gregarious bird of the thornbush country, the superb starling is commonly seen perched in treetops or feeding on the ground. Starlings have a wide vocal range and sometimes mimic other bird calls.

FOLLOWING PAGES
A vast flock of lesser flamingos inhabits Lake Nakuru. This graceful pink bird feeds in shallow water by inverting its head and unique bill, then straining allgae by pumping water out of its bill with its tongue.

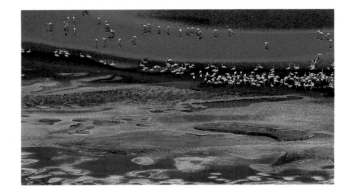

*The alkaline water of a
shallow lake would kill most
fish or mammals, but the
algae and diatoms that
thrive in the warm water
are food for the lesser
flamingo.*

*Feeding on flowering seed
heads, a yellow-bellied
waxbill moves through tall
grass near the forest's edge.*

BIRD LIFE
notes from the field

During my preparations for visiting Africa I tried to visualize the wildlife I would see and photograph, and like many people who go to Africa my expectations revolved around the large and exotic animals such as elephants, lions, leopards, giraffes, and the phenomenal herds of grazing animals. But the one category of wildlife I knew little about and was especially eager to experience was the spectacular African bird life. I had seen many photographs of some of the more typical African birds of the grasslands, such as ostriches and vultures, but I wanted to find iridescent sunbirds, jewellike fire finches and cordon-bleus, bizarre hornbills and marabous, and great flocks of flamingoes. There are over a thousand species of birds in the small country of Kenya alone, which is more than in all of North America north of Mexico, and there are probably some African species yet to be discovered. Although every bird would be new to me, I hoped to be able to apply some of my knowledge of North American birds toward finding and photographing Africa's birds.

During the first few weeks in Kenya and Tanzania I saw more than 300 species. Many of them I recognized as belonging to bird families also found in the United States. There were African fish eagles that are related to and look much like the American bald eagle, familiar-looking wading birds like squacco herons and goliath herons, and marsh harriers and other hawks, in which I recognized characteristics of North American birds of prey. The pied kingfisher, with its large head and bill, looked similar to our belted kingfisher.

But beyond the familiar there was a vast population of exotic and exciting birds. I saw six other species of kingfisher with brilliant blue and turquoise plumage and red bills. The gemlike white-throated bee eaters and the paradise flycatchers have evolved to feed on specific insect life in their rich environment, and I watched both species as they flew from their perches in short, erratic flights to catch insects in mid-air. By watching them I also found the nest and young of a paradise flycatcher in a fig tree.

The crowned crane is an elegant, royal-looking bird much different from cranes I had photographed in North America. The secretary bird is a very graceful terrestrial

*A lilac-breasted roller in
Masai Mara, perches on a
snag where it can scan the
ground for the insects and
lizards which make up its
diet.*

*An exceptionally long tail
identifies the paradise
flycatcher as it sits and
waits for insects to fly near.
In catching them,
flycatchers make short,
fluttering loops in the air.*

notes from the field *(continued)*

bird of prey with a long tail and conspicuous crest. On
Lake Nakuru, I was treated to the sight of thousands of
lesser flamingoes wading in the shallow water of the alkaline
lake, and I found darters, spoonbills, and egrets along the
shores.

Observing and photographing the birds of Africa would
be a life's work in itself. I hope to return there soon to
devote my efforts to pursuing those colorful images.

In the bush and acacia tree country, a pair of secretary birds stands on the thorny perch where they will build their nest. A terrestrial bird of prey that eats snakes and rodents, the secretary bird is the only species in its distinct family.

A small herd of beautiful impalas feeds and finds relief from the sun in the shade of an acacia. Cheetahs and leopards are their chief predators.

*Despite being abundant,
Burchell's zebras remain
one of the most striking
sights of the African plains.
Small groups and families
join together to form large
herds for protection against
predators.*

*PRECEDING PAGES
Grevy's zebras near Buffalo
Springs, Kenya, are identi-
fied by their many narrow
stripes and large, rounded
ears. At a distance, the
Grevy's zebra appears
brownish and blends into
the vegetation.*

An old termite mound is
home and vantage point for
a family of cheetahs.
Although the cheetah, the
fastest land animal, is
capable of seventy-five
miles an hour, it tires
quickly, and so it stealthily
moves within striking
distance of its prey.

Beisa oryx graze near baobab trees in Tanzania. The huge baobabs are among the longest-living plants in the world, with trunks ten feet in diameter.

The red-billed hornbill is characteristic of dry bushland and acacia country in Kenya. Male hornbills plaster the females into their nesting hollows with mud and then feed them through a small opening.

One of the more interesting inhabitants of the kopjes, the boulder and rock piles on the African savannah, is the rock hyrax. A small animal that appears to be rabbit-like, it is taxonomically the closest living relative of the elephant.

A female reticulated giraffe and her young stride gracefully across the Kenyan plains at sunset.

Papyrus growing along Lake Naivasha's shore provides a perch for a pied kingfisher watching for fish.

In the thick cover of plants around Lake Naivasha, a squacco heron waits patiently for fish to come within striking distance. Lake Naivasha is among several fresh-water lakes in Kenya that support large numbers of wading birds.

As an approaching storm darkens the sky, lions roam in Masai Mara, Kenya. Lions are the most diurnal of the large cats and often move about to set up daytime ambushes for prey.

Years of prairie wind and weather have taken their toll on a neglected barn, where a pair of sparrows seeks refuge on a cold January day.

PHOTOGRAPHY NOTES

Many times I am asked, "What kind of equipment and film do you use?" Nearly all of my photographs are made with a 35mm Nikon camera. I bought my first camera twenty years ago and the Nikon system is the one I became most familiar with; however, I do not believe it matters a great deal which camera system one uses. Great pictures are made everyday with many different cameras and lenses. What does matter is being able to respond immediately and effectively with the equipment one has at any given picture opportunity. The three most important lenses to me are the 24mm, 85mm and the 300mm. When I go into the field, I carry these lenses along with a 1.4x tele converter, and two camera bodies with motor drives. In the car, or on a major trip, I may also include an 80-200mm, a 400mm, and a 600mm lens. I would take along plenty of Kodachrome 64 for sunny days, enough Fujichrome 100 for overcast days, and a few rolls of Kodachrome 200 for days or places of little light.

Knowing the subject you intend to photograph is very important, but the subject may not always be the most important element in a picture. To me, the quality of light surrounding the subject is generally more important than the subject itself. Light gives detail, texture and mood to a scene. The best light is often thought to be that early morning or late evening "magic hour" light, but it may also be midday light filtered through fog, clouds, or the leaves of a forest.

Images with the simplest design or pattern are usually the pictures that are most personally satisfying to me. One of my favorite images—of a barn and sparrows—best sums up how the above elements come together with the actual photographic process. On a cold January 1st in 1975 while hunting pheasants in southeast Nebraska, I saw the old barn standing near the top of a hill. The light was low, but it added to the loneliness and nostalgia of the scene. I had only one camera, my first Nikon FTN, and a 55mm macro lens which is generally used for close-up photography. As I stepped into the plowed field, I glimpsed the two sparrows racing to the open door of the barn. In less than three seconds, I set the shutter speed at one five-hundredth of a second to "freeze" their flight, I estimated the corresponding f/stop of the lens, composed, focused, and pressed the shutter release.

As I conclude these final notes, I am distracted by the dozen rosy-colored Cassin's finches at the feeder, and by thoughts of how fortunate I have been to see so much. Thoughts of whales, and the animals of Africa, species of the rain forests and the old growth forests, and the birds and mammals of the Platte River and Prince William Sound. Wild, precious, delicate places. The sun is beginning to burn through the fog and a hole in the clouds reveals the fresh snow on the peaks of the Tetons. I think ahead to tomorrow and the images it will bring.